THE
WICKED WIT OF
PRINCE
PHILIP

THE
WICKED WIT OF
PRINCE
PHILIP

Compiled, edited
and introduced by

Karen Dolby

Michael O'Mara Books Limited

First published in Great Britain in 2017 by
Michael O'Mara Books Limited
9 Lion Yard
Tremadoc Road
London SW4 7NQ

A CIP catalogue record for this book is
available from the British Library.

Papers used by Michael O'Mara Books Limited are
natural, recyclable products made from wood grown in
sustainable forests. The manufacturing processes conform
to the environmental regulations of the country of origin.

ISBN: 978-1-78243-882-3 in hardback print format
ISBN: 978-1-78243-903-5 in e-book format

9 10

Designed and typeset by Tetragon, London

Printed and bound by
CPI Group (UK) Ltd, Croydon, CRO 4YY

www.mombooks.com

Contents

Introduction

*It's my custom to say something flattering to begin with
so I shall be excused if I put my foot in it later on.*

PRINCE PHILIP, SPEAKING IN 1956

Famously outspoken, Prince Philip has not always been popular with liberals. But then he's never tried to be. Always defiantly his own man, throughout a record seven decades as the Queen's consort, his gaffes have become legendary. He has been labelled reactionary, and lambasted for remarks that range from mildly crass to insultingly bigoted. He has a habit of saying aloud what others might think but never dare voice. And yet these days he is widely held in affectionate regard, attracting far more fans than outraged critics. In a world of political correctness where no one seems to say what they mean, and fake truths are considered normal, there is a refreshing directness about Prince Philip. His no-nonsense approach to life combined with his outspoken honesty and obvious devotion to the Queen is appealing. He is seen as straightforward. What you see is what you get. Plus, the man is funny.

His cousin Countess Mountbatten has said of him, 'He always speaks his mind, sometimes not necessarily with a high degree of tact. But, on the other hand, I think that people have come to expect that of him, and they really rather enjoy it and they think, how nice to hear somebody actually say what they think.'

The actor Joanna Lumley commented, 'You get the impression of meeting a bird of prey, a hawk or an eagle, there's something absolutely penetrating about the eyes, you feel like you're being scanned. You raise your game, you rather hope he'll like you.' In tribute to the Prince on his retirement, she added, 'I think he's an extraordinary character. He rides, sails, drives horses, fishes and swims and does stuff. He really could have been James Bond ... And he was a naval Commander as well. He is good fun to be around but he is quite shy. I think sometimes at some huge event I have seen him say, "Oh God, I have to do that." But then he puts his head up, chin out, and goes and does it.'

Naturalist and broadcaster Sir David Attenborough had this to say of the Prince: 'He's formidable, he's daunting, partly because of his position, but also because he is a very considerable intellect. The first time I met him, it was absolutely clear that if you turned up and you hadn't mastered the papers, he would detect it very quickly and you would be in trouble.'

In seventy years of public service, Prince Philip has been the Queen's right-hand man. On state occasions and tours, he has always been there, supporting her throughout all the ups and downs of her long reign. Their marriage is seen as the backbone of the monarchy. In a touchingly warm tribute to her husband, the Queen said on their Golden Wedding anniversary in 1997, 'He has, quite simply, been my strength and stay all these years.'

The Prince has also had his own role to play. As patron or president of more than 800 organizations and charities, he has made nearly 5000 speeches, and his varied interests include conservation and the environment, science and technology, naval history, flying, wildlife and horses, writing and painting.

Through the years he has always cut a smart figure. He appears stylishly dignified, looking as comfortable in dress uniform as he does in casual sportswear, ever since he first arrived on the public stage as the young Princess Elizabeth's fiancé. In 2016, *GQ* magazine ranked him twelfth on their annual Best Dressed list; in fact, he has been a regular on the list since it started. In the words of Dylan Jones, editor in chief of *GQ* and chairman of London Fashion Week Men's, 'The Duke is the quintessential best-dressed man, someone for whom tradition and heritage are all important. Britain needs great ambassadors and he's one of our best. And man, those suits!'

At the age of twenty-one Philip wrote to a relative, 'I am rude, but it is fun.' At the age of ninety-five, the Prince was still having fun. When news broke on 4 May 2017 that he was retiring from public duty he quipped, 'Standing down? I can barely stand up.'

Following on from *The Wicked Wit of Queen Elizabeth II*, this book focuses on the life and times of her indomitable husband, and is told through stories, anecdotes and most especially through his own unedited words. Indeed, looking back over a lifetime of memorable quotes from the Prince, it is clear that there is a great deal of knowledge, wisdom and genuine wit among the more notorious 'Philipisms' – something that he is not always given credit for.

Yet, while we may be fascinated by the Prince's gaffes, he remains nonplussed and slightly puzzled by all the fuss. 'I rather doubt whether anyone has ever been genuinely shocked by anything I have said.'

He has a remarkable ability to put people at ease, and most are charmed by his humour, even those who are the subject of the joke. With a deft word and off-the-cuff remark, Prince Philip can defuse the tension from the most formal of royal occasions, sending onlookers into fits of giggles at his latest one-liner.

'I don't think I have ever got up to make a speech … and not made the audience laugh at least once,' he said in an interview in 1999.

Timeline
of Prince Philip's Life

1921   Prince Philip is born on 10 June 1921 to Princess Alice of Battenberg and Prince Andrew of Greece at a house called Mon Repos on the island of Corfu. He is a Prince of Greece and Denmark and, as such, his name at birth is Philip Schleswig-Holstein-Sonderburg-Glücksburg. He is the youngest of five, with four older sisters.

1922   The family are forced to flee into exile following a military coup in Greece. The eighteen-month-old Philip is carried aboard HMS *Calypso*, a Royal Navy rescue ship, in an orange box. The Prince's family go to France, living in a house lent to them by his aunt, Princess Marie Bonaparte, in the Parisian suburb of Saint-Cloud.

1928   Philip is sent to Cheam School in Hampshire. While in England, he lives with his maternal grandmother, Victoria Mountbatten, at Kensington Palace, London, and his uncle George Mountbatten at Lynden Manor, in Bray, Berkshire.

1930   Philip's mother, Princess Alice of Battenberg, is diagnosed as suffering from schizophrenia and is sent to a sanatorium in Switzerland for treatment. Although she recovers, his parents live apart from this time.

1933   Philip is sent to the Schule Schloss Salem in Germany, where he stayed for two terms.

1934   Prince Philip transfers to Gordonstoun school in Scotland, which had been founded by the Schule Schloss Salem's Jewish headmaster, Kurt Hahn, who had fled from Nazi persecution in Germany. He also briefly meets the eight-year-old Princess Elizabeth for the first time at a relative's wedding.

1937   Philip's sister Cecile, her husband, two young sons and mother-in-law are all killed in a plane crash at Ostend in Belgium. She is said to be the Prince's favourite sister.

1938   Philip's uncle and guardian, George Mountbatten, Lord Milford Haven, dies.

1939   Prince Philip leaves Gordonstoun and joins the Royal Navy, becoming a cadet at the Royal Naval College in Dartmouth. In July, he meets Princess Elizabeth again. They begin corresponding regularly.

1940   Philip graduates from Dartmouth as top of his year. He is appointed Midshipman on HMS *Ramillies*, defending convoys in the Indian Ocean, then is posted to HMS *Kent* and HMS *Shropshire* in Sri Lanka. After the Italian invasion of Greece in October, he is transferred to the battleship HMS *Valiant* as part of the Mediterranean Fleet.

1941   The Prince is involved in both the Battle of Crete and the Battle of Cape Matapan and is awarded the Greek War Cross of Valour. He is promoted to Sub-Lieutenant, again achieving top marks in the qualifying exam.

1942   He is appointed to the destroyer and flotilla leader, HMS *Wallace*, and on his promotion in July, becomes the youngest First Lieutenant in the Royal Navy.

1943   As second in command, Philip devises a plan that saves his ship from a night bomber attack.

1944 The Prince moves to the Pacific Fleet on board the destroyer HMS *Whelp*. His father, Prince Andrew, dies in Monte Carlo on 3 December. Prince Philip last saw his father five years earlier.

1946 Staying at Balmoral in the summer, Philip proposes to Princess Elizabeth and asks her father's permission to marry. King George VI agrees on the condition that any formal engagement is postponed until his daughter's twenty-first birthday in April 1947.

1947 Philip renounces his Greek and Danish royal titles and becomes a naturalized British subject. He also adopts his mother's British family surname, Mountbatten. The royal engagement is announced on 9 July. The marriage takes place on 20 November at Westminster Abbey. On the morning of the wedding, Philip is created Duke of Edinburgh, Earl of Merioneth and Baron Greenwich.

1948 Prince Charles is born on 14 November. At the time, Prince Philip and Princess Elizabeth are living at Windlesham Moor, near Windsor Castle. Philip had returned to the Navy, working in the Admiralty and then at the Naval Staff College in Greenwich.

1949 The young family make Clarence House their London home on 4 July. When Philip becomes First Lieutenant of the destroyer HMS *Chequers*, the family move to the Villa Guardamangia on Malta.

1950 Philip is promoted to Lieutenant Commander in July. Princess Anne, the Princess Royal, is born on 15 August.

1951 Due to the King's continuing ill health, Philip's active naval career ends in the summer. He and Princess Elizabeth make the planned royal tour of Canada and, afterwards, they are both appointed to the Privy Council on 4 November.

1952 On 31 January, the royal couple leave Britain on a state tour. They go first to Kenya and are staying at the Treetops Hotel when Elizabeth is proclaimed Queen on 6 February upon the death of her father, King George VI. Philip breaks the sad news to his wife.

1953 Queen Elizabeth's coronation takes place on 2 June at Westminster Abbey. On 24 November, she and Philip begin a six-month tour of the Commonwealth.

1954 In May, the royal couple return home on board the newly commissioned royal yacht *Britannia* to a rapturous welcome from the British public.

1956 Prince Philip begins a six-month solo tour of the Commonwealth in the winter, prompting press speculation about the couple's marriage. They dub the trip 'Philip's Folly'. Official Palace statements to the contrary only serve to inflame the gossip.

1957 Queen Elizabeth makes Philip a Prince of the Realm.

1960 Prince Andrew is born on 19 February.

1964 Prince Edward is born on 10 March.

1969 The *Royal Family* documentary is commissioned by the Queen and Prince Philip. It is intended to give a behind-the-scenes glimpse of life at the Palace.

Prince Charles's investiture as Prince of Wales takes place at Caernafon Castle on 1 July.

1970 The first ever royal walkabout is made during the Queen and Prince Philip's visit to Australia and New Zealand.

1977 Silver Jubilee celebrations mark Elizabeth's twenty-five years on the throne. The Queen and Prince Philip become grandparents for the first time when Princess Anne gives birth to Peter Phillips on 15 November.

1981   29 July sees the wedding of Prince Charles and Lady Diana Spencer in St Paul's Cathedral. Princess Anne's second child, Zara Phillips, is born on 15 May.

1982   Prince William is born on 21 June. He becomes second in line to the throne after his father Prince Charles.

1984   Prince Harry is born on 15 September.

1986   Prince Andrew marries Sarah Ferguson in July. The couple become the Duke and Duchess of York.

1988   Princess Beatrice is born on 8 August.

1990   The Duke and Duchess of York's youngest daughter Princess Eugenie is born on 23 March.

1992   The *annus horribilis*. Scandal rocks the royal family as both the Duke and Duchess of York, as well as the Prince and Princess of Wales, announce they are to separate, while Princess Anne and Captain Mark Phillips divorce. The press is awash with embarrassing revelations. In November, a fire badly damages Windsor Castle and, as the year ends, the *Sun* leaks the transcript of the Queen's Christmas speech.

1993   Buckingham Palace is opened to the public to help pay for the repairs to Windsor Castle. A reporter for the *Daily Mirror* poses as a footman and publishes details of daily royal life.

1997   Diana is killed in a car crash in Paris on 31 August. A huge outpouring of public grief follows and her funeral on 6 September is watched by over 32 million people in the UK.

    In November, the Queen and Prince Philip attend a service of thanksgiving at Westminster Cathedral to mark their Golden Wedding anniversary and fifty years of marriage.

    The royal yacht *Britannia* is decommissioned in December after almost forty-four years of service and over a million miles travelled on official and royal duties.

2001   Prince Philip turns eighty on 10 June.

2002   Princess Margaret dies on 9 February and the Queen Mother just six weeks later on 30 March. The Queen's Golden Jubilee celebrations and tour, which begin officially in April, prove a great success and emphasize the popularity of the monarch and consort.

2005   Prince Charles and Camilla Parker Bowles are married on 9 April.

2007   Philip and Elizabeth celebrate their sixtieth wedding anniversary with a commemoration service at Westminster Abbey and a visit to Malta, where they had lived briefly as a young married couple.

2010   The couple's first great-grandchild is born: Savannah Phillips, daughter of Peter Phillips and his wife Autumn, on 29 December.

2011   Prince William and Catherine Middleton are married on 29 April in Westminster Abbey.

In June, Prince Philip celebrates his ninetieth birthday. In a televised interview he reckons he has 'done his bit' and will be slowing down. His wife gives him the title Lord High Admiral.

2012   A year of celebrations, with the Queen's Diamond Jubilee, marking sixty years on the throne, and the London Olympic Games. The Queen pays tribute to her husband, calling him her 'constant strength and guide'.

2013   Prince George of Cambridge is born on 22 July. He is third in line to the throne.

2015   Prince George's sister, Charlotte, is born on 2 May.

2017   In May, Prince Philip announces that he will be stepping down from public duty. He makes his final solo engagement on 2 August, at a Royal Marines parade, where he meets with servicemen.

'Of No
Fixed Abode'

Prince Philip first stepped into the media spotlight when he was photographed exchanging lingering glances with the young Princess Elizabeth in October 1946. They were both attending the wedding of their cousin, Patricia Mountbatten, to Lord Brabourne, at Romsey Abbey. The Prince was an usher and the Princess a bridesmaid. At the time, the press described him as a 'figure largely unknown to the British public'.

Prince Philip had been born into the Greek and Danish royal families, on 10 June 1921, on the island of Corfu. He was the youngest of five, and the only son. His parents were Prince Andrew of Greece and Princess Alice of Battenberg. The family was forced to flee into exile after a military coup in Greece placed their lives in danger. The eighteen-month-old Prince was carried on board a Royal Navy rescue ship in an orange box because they 'didn't have a cot', Philip later revealed. The family went first to France where Philip lived for seven years. He went to school there, as well as in Germany and finally in the United Kingdom.

It was an unsettled, unusual existence. 'Where was home? Wherever I happened to be. It was no great deal, I just lived my life,' he said of his dysfunctional childhood when interviewed by Fiona Bruce for the 2011 BBC documentary, *The Duke at Ninety*. 'I haven't been trying to psychoanalyse myself all the time … I'm telling you what I felt.'

By 1930, the young Prince's parents were separated. After a nervous breakdown and treatment for schizophrenia, Princess Alice retreated to a convent and when his father died in the arms of his mistress in Monte Carlo, in 1944, he had seen neither wife nor son for at least five years. Philip's inheritance was a few suits, an ivory-handled shaving brush, cufflinks and a signet ring that he still wears.

Schooldays

As his headmaster at Gordonstoun in Scotland, Kurt Hahn, said of the young Philip, 'He was one of those boys who very early rendered disinterested service and who never asked for any privilege on account of his birth.'

Speaking about his own schooldays Prince Philip said, 'I was not the least aware I was any different from any of the others. It's true I had this title of Prince, but it's surprising how you can live it down.'

Meeting the Princess

Princess Elizabeth was first briefly introduced to Prince Philip of Greece at a family wedding when she was just eight years old, but it was not until she met him in July 1939 that she really took notice. She was visiting the Britannia Royal Naval College in Dartmouth with her parents and sister for a two-day stay. Philip, a distant cousin and young cadet at the college, was asked to look after the Princesses. Dynamic, dashing and athletic, Philip caught Elizabeth's eye as he entertained her, playing games and jumping over tennis nets. A photograph from this time shows what was later to become a classic scenario. The young Princess is assiduously paying attention to whatever she was being shown, while Philip laughs uproariously in the background. When the royal party left, Philip rowed his boat after the departing Royal

Yacht, until King George yelled at him to go back. And so began a regular correspondence between the two.

Prince Philip said of the young Elizabeth, 'You were so shy, I couldn't get a word out of you.'

Their match was not altogether welcomed. Philip, though a prince, was poor and his family were scattered, and his four older sisters were all married to German princes, which remained a serious concern in the aftermath of war.

On postings to London during, and immediately after, the war, Prince Philip would stay with his grandmother, Princess Victoria, at Kensington Palace, or on a camp bed at his uncle Louis Mountbatten's home. In visitors' books from this time, he would sign himself, 'of no fixed abode'. In one visitors' book, he wrote, 'Whither the storm carries me, I go a willing guest.'

In June 1946, Prince Philip wrote to the Princess apologizing for having invited himself to Buckingham Palace. He described himself as having a 'monumental cheek ... Yet however contrite I feel, there is always a small voice that keeps saying "nothing ventured, nothing gained" – well did I venture and I gained a wonderful time.'

Later that summer, Philip was invited to stay at Balmoral by Elizabeth and it is thought that it was during his three weeks there that he proposed. Their engagement was agreed in principle but the King wanted them to wait until the Princess was twenty-one. It was announced officially on 9 July 1947.

Palace officials, meanwhile, were suspicious of the role Lord Louis Mountbatten might be seeking to play in the relationship.

The Prince wrote to his uncle warning him politely not to interfere. 'Please, I beg of you, not too much advice in an affair of the heart, or I shall be forced to do the wooing by proxy.'

And on another occasion, after the Prince and Princess's engagement had been made public, 'I am not being rude but it is apparent that you like the idea of being General Manager of this little show and I am rather afraid that she [Princess Elizabeth] might not take to the idea as docilely as I do.'

The Royal Navy

Aged eighteen, in 1939 Philip had joined the Royal Navy. He had graduated top of his year from the Britannia Royal Naval College in Dartmouth, and saw active service during the Second World War from the Indian Ocean to the Mediterranean. He was awarded the Greek War Cross of Valour and was later posted to a destroyer in the North Sea. In 1942, he became the youngest First Lieutenant in the Royal Navy.

When asked to explain his decision to join the Navy, rather than one of the other services, Prince Philip claimed, 'I didn't particularly want to go into the army. I didn't fancy walking much.'

As much as he loved being in the Navy, and enjoyed the excitement a life at sea promised, the Prince seems to have feelings as changeable as the sea itself about the ocean: 'The sea is an extraordinary master or mistress. It has such extraordinary moods that sometimes you feel this is the only sort of life – and ten minutes later you're praying for death.'

Philip's time at school in Scotland brought him his first meaningful contact with the sea, and he said of it: 'I don't think I ever thought of the sea as something to like. It's cold and wet and it's either marvellous or awful … The thing is, it's either wonderful because it looks spectacular, you see wonderful sights, but after four years of doing the morning watch I got fed up with watching the sun rise.'

A Simple Sailor

In 1950, Prince Philip was promoted to Lieutenant Commander and stationed in Malta where his wife and young family joined him. He was soon promoted to Commander but gave up his active career in the Royal Navy in 1953 to support the Queen in her royal duties. He was made Admiral of the Fleet as well as Field Marshal and Marshal of the Royal Air Force. On his ninetieth birthday in 2011, the Queen appointed the Prince Lord High Admiral, the title she had held since 1964.

'I'd much rather have stayed in the Navy, frankly,' he said in 1992 when asked how he felt about his life. Indeed, his reply when questioned about how hard it had been for him to give up a promising career in the Navy is telling: 'Well, how long is a piece of string?'

Looking back at the early years of the Queen's reign, when probed about what might have been, Philip replied: 'There was no question of my going back ... I had not thought that was going to be the end of a sort of naval career. That sort of crept up on me and it became more and more obvious that I could not go back to it. But it's no good regretting things – it simply did not happen and I have been doing other things instead.'

Lord High Admiral: The Prince on Duty

P rince of Greece and Denmark from birth, Philip renounced his titles on his engagement to Princess Elizabeth and became Mr, and then Lieutenant, Philip Mountbatten. On the day before the royal wedding, King George VI bestowed the title 'His Royal Highness' on Philip and then on the morning of the marriage, 20 November 1947, Philip was created Duke of Edinburgh, Earl of Merioneth and Baron Greenwich. It was not until 1957 that his wife made him a British Prince of the realm.

Not surprisingly, these titles brought with them an equally long list of duties. Over the decades, the Prince has made 22,219 solo engagements, aside from joint appearances with the Queen and other members of the royal family. He has accompanied the Queen on all of her 271 official overseas visits, and travelled to some 143 countries. Never one to sit idly by, the Prince has been patron or president of over 800 organizations and charities, giving up a modest dozen when he turned ninety. He is well known for his passion for conservation and as a keen sportsman. He is also fascinated by a number of other subjects including science and technology, art, history, photography and design, and is a prolific writer, with over fourteen books published.

In short, he's a busy man. And, given the sheer number of public appearances, the fact that his every move and utterance are recorded by someone, somewhere, and the Prince's outspoken, unguarded character, it is not really so shocking that there have been a number of colourful quotes or gaffes throughout his long career.

AT HOME ...

Whether at home in one of the royal residences or travelling the length and breadth of the realm on official business, Prince Philip has never been afraid of voicing his views. After so many years visiting every part of the United Kingdom, Prince Philip could be forgiven for considering himself something of an expert on British society. 'People think there's a rigid class system here, but dukes have even been known to marry chorus girls. Some have even married Americans,' he said in 2000. It has been suggested this was a veiled dig at the Duke of Windsor's marriage to Wallis Simpson but he may also have been playing to his audience of American journalists.

Getting Involved

In the early days of his wife's reign, Philip struggled to define his own position and role. Gradually, he found a number of tasks that could occupy his time. Among them was the running of Buckingham Palace, which he viewed as woefully old-fashioned, the reorganization of the Balmoral and Sandringham estates, being a ranger of Windsor Great Park, President of the National Federation of Housing Associations in the 1970s and Chairman of the Restoration Committee overseeing the rebuilding work at Windsor Castle after the 1992 fire.

'I'm, I suppose, a pragmatist. I mean, I'm here, and I might as well get on with it. There's no good saying "what if" all the time. You can't go round all your life envying other people or wishing you were doing something else,' he told the British-based American press at a lunch in December 2000.

An Interest in Industry

Philip gradually established a range of other interests and causes that he would develop over the years. In particular, the Prince has had a long association with various industrial bodies – in 1976 he started the Fellowship of Engineering, which is now the Royal Academy of Engineering, he has played an enthusiastic role in the Queen's Awards for Export and Industry, and he was President of the British Association for the Advancement of Science. His speeches throughout the 1950s and 1960s reflect his personal passion for industry and science, and he continued to champion these into his retirement.

Philip was frank about where the funding for industrial works would be likely to come from in the future: 'Princely gifts don't come from princes any more. They come from tycoons,' he said in the 1960s.

The Prince was interviewed for BBC television's *Panorama* programme on Britain's manufacturing problems in 1961. When asked why British industry was in decline Philip likened it to a national defeat 'comparable to any lost military campaign'.

While this may sound like a bleak view, in the same interview he also provided a ray of hope: 'We know perfectly well that people in this country have got a remarkable talent for things if they know how to do them.'

Prince Philip suggested to the BBC in 2015 that those were views he'd held for a while as, after the Second World War, Britain was 'completely skint – it seemed to me that the only way we were going to recover was through engineering.'

Philip also believed in the value of education. Speaking at a Royal Aeronautical Society reception in 1954, Prince Philip said, 'If a little learning is a dangerous thing then you are in for a very dangerous address … You will gather that any views I express this evening must be treated with caution if nothing else.'

At the annual lunch of the National Union of Manufacturers a year earlier, Philip opined, 'We are certainly not a nation of nitwits. In fact, wits are our greatest single asset.' Such was his conviction that his country possessed all the means at its disposal to become an industrial powerhouse.

The Prince not only focused on the macro matters of Britain's industries, but was keen to give his view on the finer points of business, too – as well as the difficulty of leveraging all of man's attributes for the best. Speaking at the 1953 NUM lunch, he said, 'Many managerial problems seem to have perfectly simple and quite reasonable solutions, but if they fail to take the cussedness of man into account these are a waste of time.'

As well as his love for science and industry, Philip also has an interest in design. From helping with the interiors of the

Royal Yacht *Britannia* to working with the Royal Mint Advisory Committee on designs for coins, seals and medals, and presenting his own award to the Designer of the Year since 1959, he has certainly got stuck in.

As President of the Royal Mint Advisory Committee, Prince Philip influenced the design of the 50 pence coin, which was introduced in 1972. 'I don't like that little "p".' As a result, it was duly changed to 'pence'. He has even personally designed pieces of jewellery for the Queen and members of staff.

> The Prince was less than impressed during an interview for ITV to mark his ninetieth birthday when Alan Titchmarsh asked which of his charities or organizations had given him most pleasure. 'It's not entertainment, I don't do it for my amusement,' he snapped.

Public Speaking

When it comes to making speeches, the Prince is a veteran. He has made almost 5000 of them on a range of subjects at all sorts of institutions, conferences and meetings. This gives an average of around eight speeches every month. Since 1952, he has been President of the English Speaking Union. The organization seeks to promote communication between countries through the English language.

'I don't think I have ever got up to make a speech of any kind, anywhere, ever, and not made the audience laugh at least once,' he has claimed with confidence in an interview with

Gyles Brandreth. 'You arrive somewhere and you go down that receiving line. I get two or three of them to laugh. Always.'

Sometimes, of course, the laughter is not always planned. 'Gratifying but sometimes unnerving is when an audience sees a joke or something amusing in a bit that was not originally intended to be funny. This happens rather more often than I care to admit,' he wrote in his 1960 book, *Prince Philip Speaks*.

In the introduction to the book, he explained his approach. 'Some people have what I can only describe as a positive genius for saying absolutely nothing in the most charming language. Neither my English nor my imagination are good enough for that, so I try to say something which I hope might be interesting or at least constructive.'

The Duke is also fully aware of the perils of delivering a speech, especially if conditions are not conducive to its successful execution. 'All sorts of unexpected things can happen in speech-making. Microphones are getting more reliable but they can still play fancy tricks. Turning a page in a high wind wearing gloves and holding a sword can also be quite exciting.'

Flying solo on a visit to Australia in 1956, Prince Philip spoke in the capital, Canberra. 'May I say right away how delighted I am to be back in Australia. The Queen and I have not forgotten the wonderful time we had here three years ago. She had to stay at home this time because I'm afraid she is not quite as free as I am to do as she pleases.'

> Prince Philip claimed he gave his best speech at the opening of the Melbourne Olympics in 1956: 'It consisted of exactly twelve words.' In fact, it was slightly longer: 'I declare open the Olympic Games of Melbourne, celebrating the sixteenth Olympiad of the modern era.' But it was delivered to rapturous applause.

The Prince always liked to do his homework if he was delivering a speech on a topic or in a location he knew little about. Speaking after dinner at the Royal Artillery Mess at Woolwich, in 1952, the Prince said, 'I am afraid I don't know much about Gunners and so before coming to Woolwich I tried to find out something. I asked the nearest soldier, but if I repeated what he said I fear I would not be asked to the mess again.'

Philip often demonstrated that, despite being born into royalty, he could still be a normal person, something he achieved with his favourite weapon: humour. Making a speech while standing in for the Queen at a Guildhall lunch in 1960, the Prince informed listeners: 'When I first heard about your invitation I was naturally flattered and grateful. For a short while I held the improbable notion that I would get a meal at the Guildhall without making a speech for it, or, at worst, a third of a speech. But I had a feeling this was too good to last and, by what I can only describe as the downright cunning of my relations, I stand before you now.'

Speaking at a Master Tailors' Benevolent Association event, Prince Philip began, 'Your president has said that the royal family have a greatly beneficial effect on your trade, and what we wear today, you wear tomorrow – I hope there will be enough to go round.'

Plain Speaking

In a speech at Edinburgh University in the late 1960s that highlighted his honesty, Prince Philip claimed, 'I get kicked in the teeth for saying things.'

In an interview for Scottish television he explained his position: 'The monarchy functions because occasionally you've got to stick your neck out ... The idea that you don't do anything on the off chance you might be criticised, [then] you'd end up living like a cabbage and it's pointless. You've got to stick up for something you believe in.' It seems that this is a philosophy he has clung to over the years.

> Philip was not unaware of his propensity to speak his mind. 'I seem to have a terrible reputation for telling people what they ought to be doing,' he once acknowledged.

Prince Philip asked a driving instructor in Oban, Scotland, in 1995, 'How do you keep your natives off the booze long enough to get them through the test?'

Being constantly on show must be wearing, and there are no doubt countless moments when Prince Philip would like to go unnoticed. However, arriving at Cambridge University in 1997 was not one of them. 'Don't you know who I am? … You bloody silly fool!' he snapped at a car-park attendant who failed to recognize him.

When asked for the secret to coping with visits and public appearances, Prince Philip was perhaps too honest. He said immediately, 'I never pass up a chance to go to the loo or take a poo.'

> Addressing an audience of industrialists
> in 1961, Prince Philip quipped, 'I have never
> been noticeably reticent about talking on
> subjects about which I know nothing.' However,
> forty-five years later he seemed to have revised
> his position, asserting, 'I don't have opinions
> about things I know nothing about.'

Damn Tourists

According to Prince Philip, speaking at the opening of City Hall in 2002, 'The problem with London is the tourists. They cause the congestion. If we could just stop the tourism we could stop the congestion.' Visit Britain, the British tourist board, not to mention the economy, might well not agree with him.

Sometimes Better to Say Nothing

In 1993, visiting survivors of the Lockerbie bombing in which 270 people died, the Prince intended to be sympathetic but missed the mark badly. 'People say after a fire it's water damage that's the worst. We're still drying out Windsor Castle.'

He also might have been wise not to enter the gun debate after the Dunblane shooting of 1996, when the murder of sixteen primary school children and a teacher had shocked the country. 'If a cricketer suddenly decided to go into a school and batter a lot of people to death with a cricket bat, are you going to ban cricket bats?'

Dontopedalogy

'Dontopedalogy is the science of opening your mouth and putting your foot in it, a science which I have practised for a good many years,' Prince Philip said in an address to the General Dental Council back in 1960.

During the Queen's Golden Jubilee celebrations in 2002, the Prince was introduced to a Sri Lankan priest. The minister was somewhat taken aback when Philip enquired, 'Are you the Tamil Tigers?' It was probably little consolation that he at least had the right country.

Wheelchairs and disability became something of a theme for the Prince during the Diamond Jubilee tour of 2012. On a visit to Bromley in Kent, Prince Philip greeted ninety-year-old Barbara Dubery who was sitting in a wheelchair, wrapped in a foil blanket as protection against the cold. 'Are they going to put you in the oven next?' he joked.

Meeting disabled mobility scooter driver David Miller, Philip enquired, 'How many people have you knocked over this morning on that thing?' Both David Miller and the gathered onlookers laughed.

Perhaps encouraged, he asked the Mayor of Waltham Forest, in east London, almost the same question, 'Have you run over anybody?' Mayor Geoff Walker has cerebral palsy, but also found the Prince funny.

Such queries were nothing new. 'Do people trip over you?' he questioned a wheelchair-bound, nursing home resident back in 2002.

On the same visit he also asked Jackie Henderson, 'Do you need a licence for that?' referring to her electric wheelchair.

Undoubtedly such blunt questions are symptomatic of an enquiring mind, rather than any intent to cause offence.

Another less sensitive enquiry came in 2008. When meeting a serviceman who had been injured by the shrapnel from an explosive device packed with ball bearings, Prince Philip asked, 'Does your head rattle?'

Philip is not any more sensitive with people closer to his own age. Visiting the Charterhouse Almshouse for elderly men early in 2017, the Prince joked to one pensioner, 'You look starved.'

> The Prince came close to the bone when he enjoyed joking with staff at a family-planning centre. Visiting the centre in April 2014, he said mischievously, 'At least you are all legitimate.'

Ironically, in the introduction to his 1960 book of selected speeches, *Prince Philip Speaks*, he had written, 'I have come to the conclusion that when in doubt it is better to play safe – people would rather be bored than offended.' Comments made since might suggest he has revised this opinion somewhat.

Working the Room

At a Leonard Cheshire Disability Charity reception held at St James' Palace in 2014, Prince Philip chatted to volunteers and supporters. He was impressed by former rugby player Alastair Hignell's hi-tech wheelchair, which could be raised or lowered as needed. 'That must be good for cocktail parties,' the Prince commented.

A short while later, he met Nikki Fox, the BBC's newly appointed disability correspondent, who was clearly anxious about meeting the Queen and Prince Philip for the first time. There's nothing like laughter for dispelling tension and leaning down to talk to Ms Fox, who was on an ordinary mobility scooter, the Prince pointed across to Alastair Hignell and said, 'You should get yourself one of those.'

The Queen was also on sparkling form at the event. Joking with Stephen Hawking, she asked whether he still had 'that American voice'. The eminent scientist quipped back, 'Yes, it's copyrighted.'

Art?

The Prince is a keen artist, and demonstrated his usual hands-on approach by suggesting the building and opening to the public of the Queen's Gallery at Buckingham Palace, converting the bomb-damaged private chapel.

However, his strong opinions naturally lead to criticisms of pieces he feels don't make the grade. A display of Ethiopian artworks in 1965 failed to impress the visiting Prince, who dismissed them as, 'The kind of thing my daughter would bring back from school art lessons.'

Dress Code

When a guest from the Chilean Embassy arrived at a reception wearing a lounge suit rather than the stipulated black tie, he got short shrift from the Prince in 1955. 'Why are you dressed like that?' Prince Philip demanded. When the man explained he couldn't afford a dinner suit and he'd been told to wear the lounge suit instead, the Prince continued, 'I suppose if they'd told you to wear a bathing suit you would have done that, too.'

Councillors for Ryde on the Isle of Wight took the royal visit very seriously in 1965. They wore their ceremonial robes for the occasion, only to be told by Prince Philip, 'You look like you are wearing dressing gowns.'

That enquiring mind was on display again when meeting Bolton council official Sean Harriss at Warburton's Bakery in 2009. Prince Philip asked, 'Are you the town clerk?' On being told that Harriss was in fact the chief executive, the Prince exclaimed, 'That's a ridiculous title. Where's your wig?'

The Prince had been chatting and joking with factory workers during the visit. Mr Harriss said, 'It is something I will remember for the rest of my life. He is famous for his sense of humour, so it is great to have shared a joke with him.'

> You can tell a lot about a person from their tie, according to HRH. In 2009 he stated, 'All original thinkers have a quality you can recognize. All architects wear ties with horizontal stripes, for instance, or no ties at all.'

Always a man with the correct look for the occasion, at a Buckingham Palace reception for IT entrepreneurs in 2014, Philip told Antony Mayfield, a digital strategy company founder, 'You can't be very successful, you're not wearing a tie.'

Perks of Office

Prince Philip has gained a reputation for not always giving due respect to authority figures. That said, few are placed more highly than royalty. In 2006, he was introduced to David MacIsaac, the newly appointed Mayor of Slough in Berkshire: 'Are you going to put on weight with all the meals you attend as Mayor?' the Prince quipped.

Meeting the Mayor again at another function a few months later, the Prince looked him up and down appraisingly. 'I told you you would get fat,' he said, patting his stomach.

Like many of those on the receiving end of the Prince's humour, Mayor MacIsaac appeared charmed, commenting, 'He is an amazing man and I hope he never changes.'

In My Day

The Prince has famously never suffered fools gladly, and he appears not to like those whose opinions fluctuate much more. Perhaps he is simply revealing a yearning for how things were in the 'good old days'.

During the 1981 recession, the Prince stated, 'A few years ago, everybody was saying we must have more leisure, everyone's working too much. Now everybody's got more leisure time they're complaining they're unemployed. People don't seem to make up their minds what they want.'

'All money nowadays seems to be produced with a natural homing instinct for the Treasury,' was the Prince's verdict on high taxes in 1963.

In 1995, he waded in with a contentious opinion on the subject of stress counselling for troops returning from active service.

Looking back at his own wartime experience he said, 'We didn't have counsellors rushing around every time somebody let off a gun. You just got on with it.'

The Armed Services

At one of the events to celebrate the sixtieth anniversary of the D-Day landings, held in June 2004, veteran soldier Tom Gilhooley was standing on parade on one of the Normandy beaches.

'You're going to pay for it, standing in this hot sun,' Prince Philip warned him. Returning an hour later, the Prince looked at the soldier's red face and laughed, not unkindly, 'I told you you'd pay for it.'

Shown a hand grenade with a mini parachute attached to it at the Defence Academy in Shrivenham, Wiltshire, in 2011, Prince Philip joked, 'I thought Heath Robinson was dead.'

A naval man he may have been, as well as a keen sailor, but one can have too much of a good thing. A tour of HMS *Boxer* in 2008 seemed to go on and on. Until the Prince exploded, 'Not another f***ing chamber!'

At the Air Training Corps in King's Lynn, in 2008, the Prince was keen to be shown some shortwave radios. 'Can you listen to anything interesting on them?' he queried. 'It doesn't get into the police network?'

Later, during the same visit, he asked a young cadet about flying in a glider, 'Have you been taken up and made to feel sick yet?'

Jumping the Queue

Accompanying the Queen, who was opening a new dental hospital in Birmingham, in 2015, Prince Philip turned to the crowd who had gathered hoping to catch a glimpse of the royal couple and said, 'Are you all here to get your teeth done? We don't want to jump the queue.'

Being Grounded

Concorde made its final transatlantic flight in 2002. The supersonic plane had become a popular icon, and many people were genuinely sorry to see it go. Though not Prince Philip. 'I must be the only person in Britain glad to see the back of that plane,' he commented. He is said to have disliked the noise it made flying over Buckingham Palace.

Although a qualified pilot who had earned his helicopter wings in 1956, he is not a fan of helicopters as a mode of transport, and in 1984 said, 'If I can persuade you to join me in this campaign, the disappearance of the helicopter is assured and then we shall be able to hold our heads high – as we march steadily back towards the caves our ancestors so foolishly vacated such a long time ago.'

At a formal lunch in the 1980s, Prince Philip was seated between his host, Ben Rosen, the head of Compaq Computers, and the general manager's wife. He found the general manager's wife far more engaging as a lunch companion and proceeded to talk to her throughout the meal, ignoring everyone else. Ben Rosen finally took advantage of a lull in the conversation and said to the Prince, 'Your Royal Highness, I understand you still fly aeroplanes.'

Prince Philip paused rather too long as he turned to look at Mr Rosen. 'Yes, you know I am in the still period of my life. That period when I can still lift a fork, still lift a glass, and still breathe,' all accompanied by the corresponding actions. 'Yes, I can still fly.'

Bang for Your Buck

The Prince believes in getting value for money. When opening the new £56 million maths centre at Cambridge University, he commented, 'This is a lot less expensive than the Dome. And I think it's going to be a great deal more useful.'

'I See You Baby'

Spotting an elderly couple sheltering from the rain beneath a Renault umbrella at a Holyroodhouse garden party in 2006, Prince Philip couldn't resist the temptation. Obviously thinking of a memorable Renault Megane TV advert in which various people shook their behinds to the song, 'I See You Baby', he walked across, waggled his own princely posterior, and asked, 'Do you do this?'

Let Me Tell You a Joke

At the Association of Chartered Certified Accountants dinner with the Queen, in 2004, Prince Philip decided that a joke was just what a room full of number crunchers needed.

'Three accountants go for a job interview and are asked to add up two plus two. The first accountant thinks for a bit and says, "Five." The second punches the numbers into his calculator and comes up with, "Four." While the third replies, "The answer can be whatever you want."'

> Reflecting the type of humour of which he is himself a fan, the organization Action on Hearing Loss gave Prince Philip a pair of ear defenders for protection when he goes shooting. The presentation was made at a reception at Buckingham Palace for his ninetieth birthday and, playing to the audience, the Prince joked, 'Can you get Radio Three on these?'

Just Another Plaque
on the Wall

The Prince has opened countless new buildings, headquarters and charitable organizations in his years of duty, and knows the form of such occasions better than anyone.

In one of his last public engagements before his retirement, Prince Philip, wearing the red and gold striped tie of the MCC (Marylebone Cricket Club), of which he is an honorary member, opened a new £25 million stand at the club's Lord's Cricket Ground. Before pulling the cord to draw aside the blue curtains, the Prince joked to onlookers, 'You're about to see the world's most experienced plaque-unveiler.'

In the early days, opening the Animal Health Trust's Farm in Essex in 1957, things didn't go quite as planned. 'Ladies and gentlemen, it gives me the greatest pleasure to declare this laboratory open ... and if someone will lend me a key I will unlock it.'

> Of all the events and commemorations the Prince has attended, he is less keen on laying inaugural stones, joking in the 1960s, 'I try to avoid laying inaugural stones because of their habit of getting lost, abandoned or stolen.'

VIP

In 1948, Prince Philip was given the Freedom of the City of London. Within the rules it states that the honour is given to 'a person of distinction'. In his acceptance speech the Prince said, 'It is always comforting to be told that one is a person of distinction. But it is even more comforting to know that it is by Act of Parliament.'

He has also been made a Freeman of the cities of Acapulco, Belfast, Bridgetown, Dar es Salaam, Edinburgh, Glasgow, Guadalajara, Los Angeles, Melbourne and Nairobi.

The Prince revealed his disdain for certain VIP traditions during a state visit to Brazil in 1968. He commented to his hosts, who had rolled out the red carpet for the royal party, 'The man who invented the red carpet needed his head examined.'

Nothing makes a man lose his sense of humour quite as badly as being made to wait when he is feeling hungry. At a dinner party in 2004, Prince Philip felt that he had been polite for long enough when he was being shown to his place at the table. 'Bugger the table plan. Give me my dinner!'

Up, Up and Away

During celebrations for the Queen's Silver Jubilee in 1977, Sir Robin Gillett, the Lord Mayor of London, was accompanying the Queen and Prince Philip up the steps of St Paul's for a service in the cathedral. It was a particularly windy day in London and the Mayor's ermine-trimmed robe suddenly filled with air and inflated like a balloon.

'Oh, look,' exclaimed the Prince, laughing uproariously. 'I think the Lord Mayor is taking off!'

Sir Robin was not in the least offended. 'I had a vision of flying up in the air like Mary Poppins, leaving the Queen and Duke behind, but his little aside helped me over a very tense moment.'

... AND AWAY

As a seasoned traveller, Prince Philip might be expected to be deft at negotiating the minefield of international relations. As it is, some of his most interesting and colourful pronouncements have been made while on the road.

Am I Tiring You?

Nigerian President Olusegun Obasanjo was dressed in an intricately embroidered *Agbada*, a traditional robe, to greet his royal guests at an elaborate formal ceremony in 2003. Prince Philip looked at his host's white costume and commented, 'You look like you're ready for bed.'

China

A certain level of tact tends to be advisable when making a royal visit abroad, although this is not always so for the Duke of Edinburgh. This was never more evident than on a trip to China in 1986, where he delivered his now-famous considered verdict on Beijing: 'Ghastly!' It should be noted that it was a judgement that he has not confined to the Chinese capital.

Later the same year he was just as critical, this time of Chinese food choices. In an address to a meeting of the World Wide Fund for Nature, the organization he co-founded in 1961, he stated, 'If it has four legs and it's not a chair, if it's got two wings and it flies but is not an aeroplane and if it swims and it's not a submarine, the Cantonese will eat it.'

It was also on this visit that he came out with what is probably his worst, most infamous gaffe. He warned a British student who was studying in China that if he stayed there much longer he would get 'slitty eyes'. It is a comment he has rightly never lived down.

Canada

In one of their early state visits in October 1951, Princess Elizabeth and Prince Philip made their first transatlantic flight to Montreal. It was the start of a thirty-five-day visit to Canada and the United States during which they would travel more than ten thousand miles, from the east coast to the Pacific and back again, by royal train. In many ways it set the pattern for all future visits. The couple tried to be as visible as possible and meet with ordinary people as well as dignitaries and officials.

Already, Prince Philip would follow behind his more serious wife, laughing and chatting to the enthusiastic crowds. It was during this trip that he made probably the first of his gaffes when he joked that Canada was 'a good investment', a remark that caused considerable offence because of its neo-colonial overtones.

Prince Philip was back stirring up more controversy on another tour of Canada and North America in 1969. Talking to an audience in Ottawa, he didn't pull any punches. 'The answer to this question of the monarchy is very simple. If the people don't want it, they should change it. But let us end it on amicable terms and not have a row. The monarchy exists not for its own benefit, but for that of the country. We don't come here for our health. We can think of other ways of enjoying ourselves.'

> Both the Queen and the Prince are fluent French speakers and have no need of an interpreter when visiting French-speaking countries. However, this did not stop Prince Philip complaining about French Canadians. 'Can't understand a word they say,' he moaned. 'They slur all their words.'

When presented with a traditional Stetson by the Mayor of Calgary in 1969, the Prince was not overly grateful. 'Not another one,' he said, but, looking on the bright side, reflected, 'Oh well, I suppose I can use it for a pot and put some flowers in it.'

Later in the day, when Philip was also given a set of antlers, the Mayor had readied himself with a few choice words: 'Don't ask me what to do with them and I won't tell you where to stick them,' he said to Philip.

> The 1969 Canadian tour was also the
> visit during which Prince Philip made
> one of his most quoted gaffes: 'I declare
> this thing open, whatever it is.'

Stateside

During a 1983 trip to the west coast of the United States, while
Ronald Reagan was president, Prince Philip was bothered by
what he regarded as over-zealous security. 'Are you expecting trouble?' he demanded of the military attaché who was shadowing
him. Hearing they were not, the Prince added, 'Then back off!'

Later in the trip he was no less prickly, and refused to switch
off the light in the royal limousine. 'Damned if I'll turn off the
light. People came to see us.'

Down Under

Despite being occasionally irritable, the Prince tends to be in good
humour on most of his foreign visits, keen to enjoy the occasion.
During a royal visit to Australia in 2002, in which the royal couple
visited some caves, Prince Philip was warned to watch out for
the drips. 'Oh,' he said breezily, 'I've run into plenty in my life.'

At a 1965 conference in Australia for future industrial and
community leaders, the Prince was asked what he had done
at the two previous conferences held in Montreal and Oxford.

'I flitted about, went to all the drinking parties, and rang a little bell sometimes.'

Travelling Hopefully

Given the decades of royal visits Prince Philip and the Queen have undertaken, it is little surprise their modes of transport have changed over time. 'If you travel as much as we do, you appreciate the improvements in aircraft design of less noise and more comfort – provided you don't travel in something called economy class, which sounds ghastly,' Philip announced to the Aircraft Research Association, in 2002.

Philip enjoys his travel – as well he might if it is all paid for by the hosts. 'I am all for people travelling at other people's expense.'

On Flying

Touching down in Canada after a long flight he was asked by a local VIP, 'What was your flight like Your Royal Highness?'

'Have you ever flown in a plane?' replied HRH, regarding the man coldly.

'Oh, yes, Sir, many times,' the eager official answered.

'Well,' said Prince Philip, moving in for the kill, 'it was just like that.'

A Prince's comfort when flying is of paramount importance. Arriving to open British Airways' new Beehive Headquarters at Gatwick Airport in December 2000, Prince Philip recalled, 'The first time I flew to Paris from Croydon Airport was in a four-seater bi-plane which travelled at 100 miles per hour and it was the size of a railway carriage. It was a great deal more comfortable than it is nowadays.'

After unveiling the commemorative plaque, the Prince chatted to cabin crew and pilots about recent air safety scares and pondered rather morbidly, 'When you think about all the publicity about planes being dangerous to fly in, I wonder, why aren't all of you dead?'

> It always pays to be prepared: as a royal visiting a foreign country, one always wants to make a good first impression. 'I usually change my trousers on the plane, otherwise I get out looking like a bag,' advised Philip.

In 2004, Prince Philip was delayed at Newcastle Airport, dressed in full Field Marshal uniform. It had been a long, tiring day. He did not wait patiently. Already standing on the tarmac, he paced up and down complaining, 'Where's my bloody aeroplane?'

Lost in Space

Knowing that the Prince was a qualified pilot, his hosts showed Philip into the control seat of a simulated space capsule on a visit to NASA headquarters in Houston, Texas, in 1991. The Prince docked the capsule and afterwards was asked what he thought of the whole experience. 'It was like a bloody great mechanical copulator,' he replied.

It is not just countries and tourists that have attracted the Prince's criticism over the past decades. When asked for his opinion of the Apollo space programme in 1968, the year before Apollo 11 landed on the moon, the Prince was not overly impressed. 'It seems to me that it's the best way of wasting money that I know of. I don't think investments on the moon pay a very high dividend.'

Island Hopping

Visiting the Cayman Islands in 1994, Prince Philip asked, 'Aren't most of you descended from pirates?'

Travelling to the Caribbean island in 2009, the Prince was presented with a pair of Bermuda shorts. 'I'm not going to put them on now,' he laughed.

'You must be out of your minds,' he told Solomon Islanders in 1982. This was after he had learned that their population growth was five per cent a year.

Visiting Malta in 2007 he rather inappropriately asked a young, engaged couple, 'How long have you two been at it?'

In Papua New Guinea, Prince Philip is addressed as 'Old fella Pili-Pili him bilong Misis Kwin' in the local creole language, Tok Pisin. On the South Pacific island of Tanna in Vanuatu, he is worshipped as the son of the local mountain god and his birthday celebrated with a feast. Over the years he has sent ceremonial clay pipes and signed photographs of himself, which have become prized possessions for the islanders. He is promised three virgin wives should he ever return.

'You managed not to get eaten then?' he joked when he met a British student who had just completed a trek through Papua New Guinea in 1998.

Globetrotting

Although he has now travelled to well over a hundred countries, back in 1967 there were still a few places he'd yet to visit. Prince Philip expressed a positive desire to visit the Soviet Union when he was asked that year if he'd consider going there: 'I would like to go to Russia very much – although the bastards murdered half my family.'

During a 1999 interview, Prince Philip was questioned if there were any countries that he had not yet visited and would like to. He was reluctant to answer openly, 'If I name them, they might invite me and then, if I couldn't make it, there'd be trouble.'

While Philip has made so many foreign visits, he has always retained a love of the country he has called home for over eight decades. Indeed, he clearly thought a group of British expats living in Abu Dhabi were mad to have chosen the hot desert climate of the Emirate state. 'Are you running away from something?' he asked.

He made a similar, less delicate, comment to an Italian tourist to Windsor Castle in 2016: 'What are you running away from? The Mafia?'

> Returning to the theme of too many tourists, the Prince told a university professor of tourism in Slovenia, in 2008, 'Tourism is just national prostitution. We don't need any more tourists. They ruin cities.'

On a royal visit to Ghana in 1999, the British Deputy High Commissioner, Craig Murray, showed the Prince a brass strip in a churchyard that marked the Greenwich Meridian line. 'A line in the ground, eh?' he murmured. 'Very nice.'

Another one of the Prince's dislikes is a bad speech. At the 2003 Commonwealth Conference held in Nigeria, Prince Philip took exception to the address made at the opening of the new British Council offices in Abuja. 'That speech contained more jargon per square inch than any I've heard for a long time,' he complained.

A short while after, he asked a group of women whether they were teachers. They answered that their job was to 'empower' people. This was too much for the Prince. 'Empower?' he spluttered. 'Doesn't sound like English to me!'

Wining and Dining

The wine cellar at Buckingham Palace is reputed to be worth over £2 million. Wines are chosen by experts and bought when young and relatively inexpensive, then allowed to mature before they are served. Since 2007, the cellars have been cooled by water from a borehole in the grounds to keep temperatures at an optimum for the bottles stored there. Prince Philip will mark the labels of wine he particularly enjoyed as 'Good' or 'Very good'.

He does, however, generally prefer drinking beer and this was obviously what he was in the mood for on a state visit to Rome in 2000. When offered a selection of fine Italian wines by Prime Minister Giuliano Amato, the Prince lost all patience and shouted, 'Get me a beer. I don't care what kind it is, just get me a beer!'

The Prince is given various gifts when visiting foreign dignitaries, and he has come to expect a certain standard. On being presented with a hamper of Southern foods by the US Ambassador Philip Lader, in 1999, the Prince rifled hastily through the contents and demanded, 'Where's the Southern Comfort?'

Those high expectations were again in evidence when, in an unflattering reference revealing his opinion of Hungarian food,

Prince Philip suggested to a British tourist in Budapest, in 1993, 'You can't have been here that long – you haven't got a pot belly.'

Award-winning French chef Régis Crépy went to great lengths to prepare a breakfast feast for the royal party in 2002. On offer were eggs, bacon, smoked salmon, kedgeree, croissants and pains au chocolat. Prince Philip was not impressed, dismissing the meal with a curt, 'The French don't know how to cook breakfast.'

At Palace banquets in the early years of the Queen's reign, Prince Philip enjoyed scrutinizing the formal menus that were often written in French, only to comment, 'Oh good – fish and chips again!'

Visiting Dublin during the Queen's historic four-day state visit to Ireland in 2011, the royal couple went to the Guinness Storehouse and watched as a pint of the brew was expertly poured. The smiling Prince could not help joking, 'Is it made with Liffey water?' He looked very tempted by the pint on offer but in the end walked away without tasting.

As a hard-working member of 'The Firm', frequently expected to make speeches and entertain, it is not surprising that Prince Philip commented cryptically in 2008, 'You find that lunches are seldom free.'

Right-Hand
Man

Until his retirement in autumn 2017, Prince Philip had stood beside the Queen for almost seventy years. He is far and away the longest serving consort in British history. Gaffes aside, he has performed this role perfectly and with great dignity, so much so that it is very easy to take his position for granted. However, at the beginning, there were no rules or job description. There was no precedent for him to follow and he had to work out his role for himself. As he approached his ninetieth birthday in 2011, when asked whether he thought he'd been successful, he was characteristically dismissive: 'I couldn't care less … Who cares what I think about it? I mean, it's ridiculous.'

What's in a Name?

Philip adopted his uncle's surname, Mountbatten, just before the official announcement of his engagement to Princess Elizabeth. Born a Prince of Greece and Denmark, he was a member of the European House of Schleswig-Holstein-Sonderburg-Glücksburg. As well as being something of a mouthful, this was considered far too Germanic in 1947, just two years after the war with Germany ended.

When Elizabeth became Queen in 1952 she initially promised her husband that their children would keep his surname, but she came under increasing pressure from Prime Minister Winston Churchill and her formidable grandmother, Queen Mary. Young and uncertain, the Queen gave in to their demands and agreed her children and grandchildren should all take the surname Windsor.

Philip was furious, ranting, 'I'm nothing but a bloody amoeba … I am the only man in the country not allowed to give his name to his children.'

Never entirely happy with her decision, in 1960 the Queen announced that any of her direct descendants who did not hold the title of Prince or Princess would be called Mountbatten-Windsor.

At the Queen's coronation on 2 June 1953, Prince Philip was the first to pay homage to the newly crowned sovereign and he solemnly promised, 'I, Philip, Duke of Edinburgh, do become your liege man of life and limb, and of earthly worship; and faith and truth I will bear unto you, to live and die, against all manner of folks. So help me God.' However, leaving Westminster Abbey after the ceremony he couldn't resist joking to his wife, 'Where did you get that hat?'

That's Life

Five years into their marriage, when they were still very much a young couple, everything changed. Elizabeth became Queen on the premature death of her father, King George VI, aged only fifty-six. Philip had given up a promising career in the Navy, resigning as Commander a year earlier when it became clear that his father-in-law was seriously ill.

Until that time, Philip recalled, 'I suppose I naturally filled the principal role. People used to come to me and ask me what to do … In 1952 the whole thing changed, very, very considerably.'

He reflected, 'There were plenty of people telling me what not to do.' However, positive guidance was in short supply. 'I had to try to support the Queen as best I could without getting in the way. The difficulty was to find things that might be useful.'

The Prince made a telling comment on his role in the royal family to the former colony of Singapore when it became self-governing in 1959: 'I have very little experience of self-government. I'm one of the most governed people you could hope to meet.'

And when asked by Gyles Brandreth in 1999 how the Prince thought he was seen, he replied, 'I don't know. Refugee husband, I suppose.'

Presenting prizes to cadets on HMS *Devonshire* in 1953, not long after cutting short his distinguished career in the Navy, the Prince said, 'I am afraid that I am in no position to offer you any advice about your future in the Navy as I only served about half a Dog Watch myself.'

Philip is on record saying of the early years of his marriage, 'The first ten years I don't remember much about.' Possibly he was referring to not recalling the details, because he did remember what the general atmosphere was like back then: 'In the first years of the Queen's reign, the level of adulation, you wouldn't believe it ... It could have been corroding. It would have been very easy to play to the gallery but I took a conscious decision not to do that. Safer not to be too popular. You can't fall too far.'

Being a member of the royal family might bring you fabulous wealth and privileges few could dream of, but Prince Philip once hinted that there are still downsides: 'We live in what virtually amounts to a museum, which does not happen to a lot of people.'

Men the World Over

Royal they may be, but in many ways, the Queen and Prince Philip are like any other long-married couple.

'Yak, yak, yak. Come on, get a move on,' Prince Philip shouted to the Queen, who was still chatting to their hosts on the quayside in Belize, in 1994. The Prince was already waiting on the deck of *Britannia*, keen to depart.

Also on board the royal yacht, the Queen is reported to have said, 'I'm not coming out of my cabin until he's in a better temper. I'm going to stay here on my bed until he's better.'

Not known for his patience generally, in the earlier years of the Queen's reign, the Prince was driving the Queen and his uncle Lord Mountbatten particularly fast. Sitting in the passenger seat, his wife grew increasingly anxious and gasped out loud a number of times.

'If you keep on doing that,' snapped Philip, 'I will stop the car and put you out.'

In 2009, the Queen and Prince were invited to the two hundred and fiftieth birthday celebrations of Kew Gardens. A large fruit cake shaped like the iconic Palm House proved remarkably difficult for the Queen to cut. Philip encouraged her noisily from the sidelines. 'Cut it properly! Press down harder!' he called, prompting a frown from his wife and the pointed suggestion that he should try, whereupon he joked, 'Let's just check if it really is a cake because sometimes they aren't.'

When asked for his recipe for a successful marriage in 1997, Prince Philip didn't hesitate: 'Tolerance is the one essential ingredient ... You can take it from me the Queen has the quality of tolerance in abundance.'

He is also quoted as saying that the 'ideal arrangement' is to have a wife to 'keep, groom and train the ponies'. While this is a somewhat outmoded view – one assumes the Prince made it with tongue firmly in cheek – it has to be said that the Queen is known to be an excellent horsewoman.

Second Fiddle

At a reception to honour Australians, Philip met Joe Kerr, the British husband of Australian Gill Hicks, who lost her legs in the July 2005 London bombings. 'You're not Australian!' the Prince exclaimed.

Joe Kerr replied, 'No, actually, I'm not important. I'm just here because of my wife.'

'Tell me about it!' Philip sympathised.

On another occasion, visiting an Australian university, the Prince was introduced to Mr and Dr Robinson. Mr Robinson explained, 'My wife is a doctor of philosophy and much more important than I am.'

'Ah yes,' nodded Prince Philip. 'We have that trouble in our family, too.'

Discussing his position in an interview with Jeremy Paxman, Philip was characteristically dismissive, commenting, 'Any bloody fool can lay a wreath at the thingamy.'

> Prince Philip explained his role to Michael Parker, his first private secretary, in no uncertain terms: 'My job, first, second and last is never to let the Queen down.'

The Queen paid tribute to her husband's sense of duty at a Guildhall lunch in 1997, celebrating their Golden Wedding anniversary: 'He is someone who doesn't take easily to compliments. He has, quite simply, been my strength and stay all these years, and I, and his whole family, and this and many other countries, owe him a debt greater than he would ever claim or we shall ever know.'

Mysteries of Monarchy

It is sometimes far better to accept one's lot than to query tradition. Back in 1960, when asked about the ceremony of Trooping the Colour that takes place each year on a Saturday in June to mark the Queen's official birthday, the Prince shrugged and said, 'Don't ask me to explain why it is that she has an official birthday in June when her proper birthday is in April. You'll just have to accept it like cricket, pounds, shillings and pence, and other quaint, but quite practical, British customs.'

Mr and Mrs

The Queen and Prince Philip also share a few in-jokes. Their nickname for the line-up of dignitaries who greet them on official visits is the 'chain gang'. This is a reference to the chains, hats and robes often worn by mayors and their deputies.

Given his sense of humour, it is no surprise that Philip enjoys teasing his wife. Sitting next to the Queen at the Royal Variety Show in 2014, about to watch the final male stripper scene from the stage version of *The Full Monty*, the Prince reassured his biographer Gyles Brandreth, 'Don't worry, she's been to Papua New Guinea and seen it all before.'

Years earlier, when introducing the biographer to the Queen and explaining that Brandreth was going to write about her, Prince Philip added with relish, 'Be warned, he's going to cut you to pieces.'

On a visit to Canada, crossing to Vancouver Island, stormy weather rocked the royal ship just as a young officer attempted to serve them afternoon tea. A tray of cakes crashed to the floor, whereupon Prince Philip helped pick them up. Sitting back down next to his wife he quipped, 'I've got mine. Yours are down there.'

In 2015, Prince Philip accompanied the Queen on a visit to Southampton where she was to name the new P&O cruise liner *Britannia*. During the visit the Queen was asked to sign an empty picture mount in which a photograph of herself would later be placed to hang on board the ship. Watching his wife sign the blank frame, the Prince joked, 'It's not a very good likeness, is it?'

> It is to be assumed that Prince Philip was being flippant when asked for his thoughts on making the Queen's annual Christmas message more entertaining. 'Short of hiring a line of chorus girls and calling it *The Queen Show*, what can you do?'

While Philip does enjoy some gentle ribbing of his wife, he is always there to look out for her. In 1954, on their first big tour of Australia and New Zealand, the protocol and rigours of state visits were still new to the Queen. The constant crowds and searing heat were overwhelming and she began to look thoroughly miserable. Prince Philip appeared at her side and said, 'Cheer up, sausage.'

The royal couple, like any other couple, do make public displays of affection. Upon returning from his first official solo tour of the Commonwealth in 1957, the Prince, sporting an impressive newly grown beard, was met by the Queen and greeting party, who were all wearing false ginger beards. To mark the many weeks apart, Philip wore a heart-decorated tie.

When they are apart, the Prince rings his wife every evening to chat about the day's events, and his affectionate names for her include 'cabbage' and 'sausage'.

> When the *Oldie* magazine voted him
> 'Consort of the Year' in February 2011, the
> Prince wrote in a letter to them, 'There is
> nothing like it for morale to be reminded that
> the years are passing – ever more quickly – and
> that bits are dropping off the ancient frame.
> But it's nice to be remembered at all.'

Don't Scare
the Horses

Never a fan of inactivity, Prince Philip could be described as a sports enthusiast, and among the 800-odd organizations of which he has been patron, sporting ones feature prominently. From schooldays at Gordonstoun, he has played football, hockey, rugby, cricket, badminton and squash. As an adult he has been a keen yachtsman and became Admiral of the Royal Yacht Squadron and President of the Royal Yachting Association as well as sailing regularly at Cowes Week Regattas. He took his first flying lesson in 1952, receiving his Royal Air Force wings the following year. He is probably most associated in the public's mind with polo playing and carriage driving. While a keen rider, the Prince is less enamoured of horse racing and has been known to hide a radio in his top hat when attending Ascot in order to listen to the cricket. Generally, he would rather take part than watch: 'I'm not really a talented spectator, frankly … I'd rather do something.'

He generally values the competition inherent in most sports. 'Everything you do is based on competition unless some half-witted teacher seems to think it's bad for you. People like to pit their abilities against someone else. People want to race each other. It's what gives the whole thing spice.'

The Sport of Kings

In 1965, Prince Philip famously claimed, 'The only active sport I follow is polo and most of the work is done by the pony.'

However, he obviously took the sport very seriously. He refused an opportunity to play in Pakistan saying, 'I went to Pakistan on serious business. If I'd gone there to play polo I'd have got in some practice beforehand.'

After one match that hadn't gone as well as he would have liked, he complained that polo umpires were 'mutton-headed dolts totally ignorant of the simplest rules of the game'.

Albeit mockingly, the Prince hinted at the importance polo has for him when speaking on US television in 1969 about the royal family's finances: 'We go into the red next year … I shall probably have to give up polo.'

In fact, the Prince eventually gave up playing in 1971, taking up carriage driving a couple of years later because it was, he thought, the perfect sport for middle age.

Horses and Carriages

The Prince's next sporting passion was a logical choice. 'I gave up polo when I turned fifty and then this started and I thought, "Well, you've got horses and carriages, why don't you have a go?" So I started in 1973 and it's been going on since then. These were carriage horses from London – they'd never been through anything bigger than a puddle. I made a little crossing – a stream – and had to bribe them across. I sent my groom across the other side with a jar of sugar and they decided to get their feet wet!'

He also claimed, slightly implausibly, given his character, 'I took it up as a geriatric sport. I thought of it as a retirement exercise. I promise you, when I set out I thought it would be a nice weekend activity, rather like a golfing weekend. Which it was until some idiot asked me to be a member of the British team.'

Indeed, the Prince turned out to have a genuine talent for the sport. 'In 1973 I entered my first national competition and to my horror I was told I could compete in the European Championships in May that year as an individual. I did, and I was rather impressed. Things went quite well until I hit the last obstacle, which damaged the carriage to such an extent I had to retire before the end. However, I had a clear round in the cones so I was not last, at least.'

The Prince obviously enjoyed the competition but after hitting a tree and overturning his carriage in a 1974 race he was not in the best humour. Asked if he enjoyed the sport, he snapped, 'Don't be a fool! Do you think I do it for penance?' His temper was stretched further when the interviewer queried whether he had another team of horses available, sneering, 'Another team? Do you think they grow on trees?'

> When asked whether carriage driving got in the way of his official duties, the Prince replied, 'It's the other way around. The duties get in the way of the driving.'

The Prince remains the longest serving President of the International Equestrian Federation, holding the position from

1964 to 1986. He was responsible for drawing up the rules for competitive carriage driving and was a member of the British gold-medal winning teams at the World Championships in 1974 and 1980.

When asked about protocol for carriage driving by a Chinese delegate, the Prince was remarkably casual: 'As far as we are concerned, you can play "Colonel Bogey" and fly a pair of knickers from the flagpole as your team enters the arena.'

> Prince Philip has amused spectators with his colourful outbursts while driving, yelling, 'Come on, you bloody idiots!' to encourage his horses on more than one occasion.

Writing in his book *Men, Machines and Sacred Cows*, which was published in 1984, Prince Philip had this to say about horses: 'The horse is a great leveller and anyone who is concerned about his dignity would be well advised to keep away from horses. Apart from many other embarrassments there is, for instance, no more ridiculous sight than a horse performing its natural functions with someone in full dress uniform mounted on its back.'

> Asked at the age of eighty-five whether he would be riding in the Trooping the Colour procession the next day, he smiled and said, 'No, I'm not. The horse is too old.'

As he reached his mid-sixties, the Prince decided to swap horses for rather less powerful ponies. Come his mid-eighties, he conceded, 'You'd be surprised how much work it is. You've got to practise like mad and it's absolutely bloody exhausting.'

Not to mention frustrating. He admitted after less than successful days that 'I want to shoot the lot of them. Then myself.'

When journalist Sue Mott, interviewing him for the *Daily Telegraph*, had the temerity to point out the dangers of the sport for someone of his advanced years and position, the Prince reacted forcefully. 'You haven't got a bloody clue, have you? You've never seen anybody come to any harm, so why do you say it's dangerous? It's like climbing. People say, "Oh, you can fall off." Well they don't fall off. Not if they learn properly and if they're properly organized.' He felt it was only 'dangerous for people who don't know the first thing about it'.

Danger can come in many forms, however. After competing in Hungary, in 2004, he commented, 'The most dangerous part of that tournament was visiting the Hungarian camp because whatever the time of day, they gave you a glass of peach brandy and you were lucky to escape with your life.'

Even in his mid-nineties, it is not unusual to spot the Prince driving a carriage through Windsor Great Park, these days accompanied by two grooms and well wrapped up against the elements. In his book *30 Years On and Off the Box Seat*, he explained, 'When I started driving, I used to try to find people I could stay with so that I could drive. I now drive so that I can go and stay with people.'

But what of the future? 'I have been fortunate to have had a longer innings than most, and I have no intention of giving up while I have a team of willing ponies and dedicated staff and while I can still cope with the challenges which carriage driving presents me with,' he wrote.

Football

Although President of the Football Association in the 1950s, the Prince does not always seem to be the biggest football fan.

At Highbury Stadium, meeting a member of Arsenal's celebrity team who was wearing a replica shirt with the sponsor's name, Sega Dreamcast, printed on it, Prince Philip asked, 'Is Dreamcast the name of the team?'

Visiting Nottingham Forest Football Club, Prince Philip pointed to the club's trophies and enquired, 'I suppose I'd get in trouble if I were to melt them down?'

On a 1962 visit to Uruguay, the Prince stated, 'I am convinced that the greatest contribution Britain has made to the national life of Uruguay was teaching the people football.'

History is another of the Prince's passions so it is unsurprising that he should know something of football's past. 'Henry VIII is supposed to have joined in a game during a recruiting march. He ultimately emerged with a torn shirt and all the players enlisted in the army ... One of the Jameses was ordered by his father not to play any more, either because of the clothes bill or more probably because every time he appeared in public people wondered why he had a black eye.'

On Cricket

Prince Philip is one of the royal family's keenest cricket fans. He was a talented player and at school was captain of the Gordonstoun cricket XI. He has served as President of the MCC twice, in 1949 and 1974, and is an honorary life member. He is also the honorary twelfth man and patron of the Lord's Taverners, the actors' cricketing charity that meet at the Tavern pub at Lord's Cricket Ground.

In a preface to a 1962 book the Prince wrote, 'I cannot claim to have an intimate knowledge of the Lord's Tavern but I do know that it has an atmosphere that cannot be ascribed to cricket alone! Quite what it is that makes the Tavern such a very special place, I don't know ... Just cricket? Scientists one day may discover what controls the homing instinct of fish and birds but I hope they never try to analyse the urge of the Taverner to return to Lord's.'

After opening a new stand at Lord's, in one of his last-ever official public engagements in May 2017, the Prince was shown a selection of historic cricket bats including a huge, baseball-style bat with an extra-long handle that is now ruled illegal. He joked to former England cricket captain Mike Gatting, 'It's an offensive weapon.'

Prince Philip told England Women's Captain Clare Connor that her Ashes trophy 'Looks like something cobbled together in a sixth-form woodwork class.'

Addressing a cricket club conference, Prince Philip said, 'The last time I played in a village match I was given out LBW first ball. That is the sort of umpiring that should be looked into.'

Interviewing the Prince for a Test Match Special, commentator Brian Johnston asked how modern cricket could be improved. Philip replied, 'I only wish to God that some of their trousers fitted better.'

On a visit to Lord's Cricket Ground in 2009, Prince Philip asked Tim Nielsen, the Australian head coach, 'Are you the team's scorer?'

The Prince was clearly getting into his stride. The same day an MCC official enquired whether he had enjoyed his lunch. 'Why do you ask that?' Philip wondered.

'I hoped the answer would be yes,' the official replied.

'What a stupid question,' the Prince retorted.

Any Sport Will Do

While sailing at Cowes, a crewman on board an approaching yacht shouted to Prince Philip, 'Water!' (which in yachting parlance, means move out of the way) adding, 'Stavros!'

The Prince yelled back, 'It's not Stavros and it's my wife's f***ing water, so I'll do what I f***ing please!'

While Prince Philip's fondness for sailing is no surprise, slightly less expected is his interest in tiddlywinks. Students from Cambridge University challenged him to a tiddlywinks match after the *Spectator* published an article entitled 'Does Prince Philip Cheat at Tiddlywinks?' in 1957. He accepted the challenge and appointed the Goons as his royal champions.

He has awarded 'The Silver Wink' to the winner of the Inter-University Tiddlywinks Championship every year since 1961.

The Prince may be one to rise to a challenge. He was not, however, keen to try bungee jumping. When asked in 2006 whether he had ever considered the sport, which was invented on Vanuatu where he is considered a god, Philip said, 'No. I don't think I'd like my eyeballs to go out and then in again, somehow.'

> Meeting Eddie Jordan, the BBC Formula One presenter and former Jordan team boss, the Prince exclaimed with a flash of recognition, 'Ah! You're that funny chap who does the F1!'

When introduced to David Walliams, who had just swum the English Channel for Sport Relief in 2006, the Prince seemed less than impressed.

'Is this the nut who swam the Channel?' he asked before turning to the comedian's mother and saying, 'Are there any more nuts in your family?'

The Olympics

Speaking at the Helsinki Games in 1952, the Prince said, 'It's much more important to come away from the Olympic Games with a good reputation and having made friends with everybody there than to come back with a bagful of medals. On the other hand, I have no objection to doing both.'

When asked what he would be doing at the 2012 London Olympics, the Prince replied, 'As little as possible.'

Looking at the number of gold medals on display at a Buckingham Palace reception for British Paralympians in 2009, the Prince remarked, 'There is so much gold in the room some should be donated to Gordon Brown to help ease the country's cash crisis.'

> At a golfing dinner in 1949, Prince
> Philip began his speech with, 'Prepare
> for a shock. I do not play golf.'

In America

Prince Philip was keen to get involved with sport when on his travels, too. On a state visit to New York and Washington in 1957 where the royal couple were entertained by President Eisenhower, he said, 'We watched a game [of American football] in America last week. I can't say it is a close relation to soccer but it's fascinating to watch and it's more like a campaign than anything else.'

During the same visit, on a ferry crossing the Hudson River in New York, Prince Philip pointed at the Brooklyn skyline. 'That has a famous baseball team, doesn't it?'

'Yes, Sir. We call them the …'

Philip finished for him. 'I know, you call them "dem bums".'

Green But
Slightly Mean

Passionate about conservation, the Prince has written a number of books on the subject. He was the first President of the World Wildlife Fund in the UK from its beginnings in 1961 until 1982, President of WWF International from 1981 until 1996 and is now President Emeritus of the organization, now known as the World Wide Fund for Nature. Nevertheless, he would never describe himself as 'green' and in his own words is certainly 'no bunny hugger'. In Fiona Bruce's BBC interview to mark his ninetieth birthday, Prince Philip expanded on his views. 'If we've got this extraordinary diversity on this globe it seems awfully silly for us to destroy it. All these other creatures have an equal right to exist here, we have no more prior rights to the Earth than anybody else and if they're here let's give them a chance to survive.' He went on to explain, 'I think that there's a difference between being concerned for the conservation of nature and being a bunny hugger – people who simply love animals.'

The Prince is also the founder of the ARC, the Alliance of Religions and Conservation, which supports the work of religions around the world in protecting the environment. He worked with the charity for over thirty years until he stepped down from official duties in 2017. His standpoint was clear: 'If you believe in God … then you should feel a responsibility to care for his Creation.'

This does not mean that the Prince is not also a keen shot and a vocal advocate of blood and field sports.

Always outspoken in his views, he has ruffled more than a few feathers over the years.

Speaking His Mind

Although happy to accept a conservation award in Thailand in 1991, this did not stop the Prince from going on to criticise his hosts in his speech: 'Your country is one of the most notorious centres of trading in endangered species in the world.'

Long before conservation became the popular norm, Prince Philip condemned African poachers who hunted rhinoceros for their horns, a popular ingredient in traditional Chinese medicine. Speaking in New York in 1962, he said, 'For some incomprehensible reason, they seem to think it acts as an aphrodisiac. They might as well grind up chair legs.'

Conservation and the Environment

Over the years, Prince Philip has worked tirelessly for the World Wild Fund for Nature and has visited WWF projects in more than forty countries on five different continents. Explaining the organization's mission as the charity's president, he quipped, 'We have no intention of campaigning against mousetraps or flypapers.'

The Prince would demonstrate his interest in the preservation of the natural world in whatever setting he found himself. He undoubtedly only had the conservation of animal habitats on his mind when, at a WWF event in 1993, he asked fashion writer Serena French, 'You're not wearing mink knickers, are you?'

Philip could sometimes become annoyed at how people who proclaimed themselves to be conservationists or 'green', in his view, failed to focus on the real issues. 'People are more concerned about how you treat a donkey in Sicily than conservation,' he told Fiona Bruce when interviewed in June 2011.

Killer Cats

While Philip cares deeply for the environment and the equal rights of all animals, he is famously less than fond of one particular creature. The Prince made his opinion of cats very clear when visiting a project for the protection of turtle doves in Anguilla in 1965. 'Cats kill far more birds than men. Why don't you have a slogan: "Kill a cat and save a bird"?'

His opinion hadn't shifted forty years later: 'People don't like to admit it but cats catch an enormous number of small wild birds. But people are very attached to their cats – it's a fact of life.'

Bird Book

Prince Philip is a keen birdwatcher and was patron of the British Trust for Ornithology from 1987 until his retirement. Two interests collided when he published a book of his bird photography called *Birds from Britannia* in 1962, which was a record of his travels during the late 1950s. In the introduction he wrote, 'The photographs are in black and white simply because I prefer taking photographs in black and white. Fortunately, most of the birds themselves are black and white, or grey anyway, so not much is lost.'

Some years later he reflected, 'I have had two books of speeches published, and one on birds. Needless to say, the one on birds was more successful.'

Bear Necessities

Koala bears may look cute and cuddly, but this was not enough to entice the Prince to risk stroking one on a visit to Australia in 1992. He firmly declined, 'Oh no. I might catch some ghastly disease.'

During a discussion on the difficulties of encouraging pandas to breed in captivity, it was suggested that the animals were reluctant to mate because they became too attached to their keepers. Prince Philip had a simple answer: 'Well then, the logical solution would seem to be to dress one of the pandas up as a zookeeper so that the other one fancies it.'

> On tour in Anguilla in 1994, the Prince had an unusual piece of advice to offer islanders: 'Don't feed your rabbits pawpaw fruit – it acts as a contraceptive. Then again, it might not work on rabbits.'

Get It Right

'I do like your tree fern,' Prince Philip said to gardener Jamie Durie at the 2008 Chelsea Flower Show.

'Actually, it's not a tree fern, it's a member of the cycad family … a *Macrozamia moorei*,' Durie replied.

'I didn't want a bloody lecture,' the Prince snapped, turning on his heel.

A Bloody Business

Unsurprisingly, the Prince has strong views on sports involving animals, which some have found hard to reconcile with his belief in conservation and concern for animal welfare.

'Fox hunting is a curious thing to ban because, of all the blood sports, it's the only one where the people following it don't come anywhere near a wild animal at all.'

He has also compared field sports (hunting, shooting and fishing) to a butcher's work, managing to offend fairly widely in doing so. 'I don't think doing it [butchering animals to sell as meat] for money makes it any more moral. I don't think a prostitute is more moral than a wife, but they are doing the same thing. It is really rather like saying it is perfectly all right to commit adultery providing you don't enjoy it.'

'Can't you think of anything else to say?' was his terse response to an animal rights demonstrator at Cambridge University in 2003, who was shouting slogans at him through a megaphone.

Don't tell Charles ...

After a meal of venison at Magdalen College, Oxford, to celebrate the five hundred and fiftieth anniversary of its foundation, Prince Philip pointed to the herd of deer grazing in the grounds and asked the bursar, 'How many of those buggers did you have to shoot for lunch, then?'

The bursar looked shocked. The college's deer are much prized and the venison consumed that day had come from Kent.

'Well, don't tell Charles,' the Prince joked. 'Because he likes everyone to buy local.'

Farming Today

Conservation has a strong correlation with farming and the techniques used in agriculture and managing livestock. The Prince's views on farming methods have sometimes been challenged.

When interviewed by a farming magazine and asked if conservation was not too important an issue to be left to conservationists, Prince Philip had no hesitation in replying, 'I would say that farming is too important to be left to farmers.'

He echoed this opinion when three employees of a Scottish fish farm met the Prince at Holyrood Palace in 1999. 'Oh!' Philip declared accusingly. 'You are the people ruining the rivers and the environment!'

In an interview for *Shooting Times*, the Prince was even more critical of modern farming practices. 'They are constantly trying to produce cattle that will produce more milk and less cow, like a hat rack with an udder attached. They can't really go on making such a travesty of an animal, there must be a limit to this. Even more ridiculous is the fact that milk is actually cheaper than bottled water. It seems quite bizarre to me.'

At a Diamond Jubilee garden party at
Buckingham Palace in 2012, the Prince
discussed continental cattle with a farmer.
He grinned before commenting on European
beef, 'Oh, that awful tasting thing.'

Breeding Like Rabbits

The problems of population growth and overpopulation have
long been a concern of Prince Philip.

Back in 1968 he had suggested a 'tax on babies' as a remedy
for this, although he later claimed this was a joke. He is, however,
an advocate of birth control. 'You can't expect to go on a bender
and not expect a hangover.'

Philip is adamant that the human population is directly responsible
for more than food shortages and rising prices, and that it has
had a sometimes catastrophic impact on the natural world.

Perhaps this prompted his rather eccentric solution to tackling
the problem. 'In the event that I am reincarnated, I would like
to return as a deadly virus, in order to contribute something to
solve overpopulation,' the Prince was quoted as saying in 1988.

Twenty years later he was a little more circumspect: 'It's
embarrassing and no one knows how to handle it, because
nobody wants their family life to be interfered with by the
government.'

It's an Ill Wind

Although the Queen and Prince Philip have introduced a number of green initiatives at the royal residences, including setting up hydropower turbines on the River Thames to generate the electricity for Windsor Castle, the Prince is vehemently opposed to wind power.

'When they put up a whole farm of windmills off the north-east coast of Norfolk, which is on the main [bird] migratory route to Scandinavia, are we going to get sliced up ducks coming across?'

In 2011, he told the owner of a wind turbine company that wind farms were 'absolutely useless' and an 'absolute disgrace', summing up his argument with, 'You don't believe in fairy tales, do you?' and a warning, 'You stay away from my estate!'

Opening the Fasnakyle Hydroelectric Power Station in the western Highlands of Scotland in 1952, Prince Philip said, 'To suggest that the power station alone destroys the beauty of Glen Affric is being as fastidious as the fairy tale princess who could feel a pea under fifteen mattresses.'

Not in Front
of the Children

One of Prince Philip's best-known associations is with the Duke of Edinburgh Award Scheme, which was founded by the Prince in 1956 and has benefited more than 7 million young people worldwide since it started. Talking about the scheme in an interview in 2011, the Prince was modest about his achievements. 'I've no reason to be proud. It's satisfying that we've set up a formula that works but I don't run it. It's all fairly second-hand … I didn't want my name attached to it. That was against my better judgement. I tried to avoid it but I was overridden.'

While he often ignores or rides roughshod over due credit and praise, Philip continued his involvement with the Duke of Edinburgh Award Scheme – and a number of other schemes and activities aimed at children – for many years, naturally bringing him into contact with the younger generations. Over the years it has become abundantly clear that the Prince is no more guarded in his dealings with young people than with anyone else.

And the Award Goes to …

Despite the great achievements of the Duke of Edinburgh Award Scheme, its success did not always seem to lift his spirits. In 2006, at a Buckingham Palace reception marking the scheme's fiftieth anniversary, the Prince was in a reflective mood. 'We get a small government grant and I sometimes wonder, why bother? … You sell your soul to the government and that's it.'

The same year, he was also asked whether he thought the scheme was still as relevant as when it was first set up. 'Young people are the same as they always were. They are just as ignorant.'

It's always nice to meet a fellow traveller. Meeting young participants in 2008's Award Scheme, one told the Prince he had been doing conservation work in the jungle of Belize, the same place the SAS trained. Prince Philip smiled and said, 'It's a lovely part of the world; a bit like Sussex in places.'

When asked in 2001 whether he thought the Duke of Edinburgh Award scheme would have been even more popular if it had a different name, he replied, 'Whatever you call it, some people will think it is rubbish while some people would not be worried about this connection with this cantankerous old sod.'

Teaching Standards

The Prince made various visits to schools during his career, and has his own ideas of how education should be carried out.

Visiting the Samuel Whitbread Community College in Bedfordshire, the Prince looked in on a science class.

'Is there any sign of intelligent life in this classroom?' he asked.

Surprised teacher Wendy Hill stuttered, 'I wouldn't know.'

'Well, you should know!' reprimanded the Prince.

The teacher later said she considered it 'a privilege to have been so soundly ticked off by Prince Philip. It made my day.'

The Prince's fixed ideas on schooling, which may explain his sometimes brusque demeanour with schoolchildren, perhaps were influenced by his own education. 'Children may be indulged at home, but school is expected to be a Spartan and disciplined experience in the process of developing into self-controlled, considerate and independent adults.'

Visiting Crawley with the Queen in 2006, Prince Philip stopped at the library of Thomas Bennett Community College for middle-school children. He asked teacher Judith Jarvis, 'Can they all read?' The surprised teacher replied that they could, which appeared to amuse the Prince enormously.

Higher Education

Having not gone to university himself, Philip didn't always hold higher education in the greatest esteem and enjoyed poking fun at it whenever the opportunity arose. He was certainly no respecter of the grand educational institutions. He commented on universities, 'The first five hundred years of any institution are always the most difficult.' The Prince said to a group of students of his own education, 'I am one of those stupid bums that never went to university and a fat lot of harm it did me.'

He echoed these sentiments at the University of Salford, where he declared, 'The best thing to do with a degree is to forget it.'

His philosophy on the usefulness of
university was a simple one: 'University is
merely so much vocational training unless
it puts some fire in your belly.'

Having had a rather privileged life himself, it is interesting to hear
his thoughts on privilege in education. 'Up to quite recently, it
was thought one gets into a university by paying, but now there is
another privilege – intellectual privilege, which is another mistake.
Privilege is privilege whether it is due to money or intellect or
whether you have six toes.'

'In education, if in nothing else, the Scotsman knows what is best
for him. Indeed, only a Scotsman can really survive a Scottish
education.' This remark was made when Prince Philip became
Chancellor of Edinburgh University in November 1953. It's
worth remembering that he was himself a pupil at Gordonstoun,
in Moray, north-east Scotland, an experience he so enjoyed that
he sent all three sons to the school.

The Prince was honest about his own schooldays. Looking back,
he said, 'My favourite subject at school was avoiding unnecessary
work.' His attitude must have changed, given the lifetime of
service and public appearances he went on to make.

The Prince has often been rather amused by certain regional accents. At the University of Salford in 2012, Prince Philip met a student from Manchester and another from Liverpool. 'Do you fight?' he asked. On being joined by a Sheffield student with a pronounced accent, he continued, 'Do you understand each other?'

In the same vein, it's hard to know who should have felt the most insulted when he said of students from Brunei arriving to study in 1998, 'I don't know how they're going to integrate in places like Glasgow and Sheffield.'

Philip has always been one to offer advice, even if it is advice he may never have had to take himself. 'Why don't you go and live in a hostel to save cash?' This was Prince Philip's considered counsel to a young, penniless student, worried about racking up a sizeable student debt.

On a 1961 visit to Sheffield Hallam University, the Prince was shown a plastic dummy used for medical training, which lay in bed saying, 'I don't feel well.'

'Frankly, you don't look well,' Prince Philip quipped.

In a speech to overseas students on the art of after-dinner speaking, Prince Philip was entertaining. 'It makes the job of the speakers so much easier if the audience is somewhat "mellowed". Conversely, it makes the speeches so much more tolerable – or, of course, if you have gone beyond a certain point, it makes them irrelevant, or sometimes even inaudible.'

Open and Shut

Opening university departments has been something of a speciality for the Prince throughout his career.

Unveiling a plaque at the University of Hertfordshire's new Hatfield Campus in 2003, Prince Philip made a short speech, 'During the Blitz a lot of shops had their windows blown in and sometimes they put up notices saying, "More open than usual." I now declare this place more open than usual.'

Forgetting his vast experience of unveiling plaques, Philip said in the 1990s, 'My only claim to fame is that I'm the most experienced visitor of technological facilities. I've been doing it professionally for forty years. I can claim to have petted the first microchip on the head.'

Occasionally, the Prince missed the obvious. 'It doesn't look like much work goes on at this university,' he was overheard commenting at the Engineering Faculty at Bristol University. In fact, the department had been specially closed so that the Queen and Prince Philip could officially open it in 2005.

At the opening of an extension to Heriot-Watt College in Edinburgh, in 1958, the lift transporting the royal party became stuck between two floors – a gift for Prince Philip who found it highly amusing. 'This could only happen in a technical college,' he laughed.

Hair Today

It wasn't just schoolchildren and students who were in the Prince's educational firing line. On a Golden Jubilee visit to the University of East London, Prince Philip was introduced to a member of staff who was not a lecturer. 'That's right,' the Prince said. 'You do not have enough hair to be a lecturer.'

On the same visit, the Prince was taken to see an air-flushing environmentally friendly toilet, asking, 'Where does the wind come from?' When shown the pellets of sewage and ash that were produced from sewage recycling he joked, 'What do they eat in East London to get that?'

Watching a fashion show in East London, he met those involved afterwards with the Queen. 'Your hair is too long. You should get it cut for the fifties,' he told model Somonah Achadoo.

Honorary Degrees

The Prince has been awarded a vast number of honorary degrees, titles and chancellorships over the years. His first degree was a Doctorate of Law from the University of Wales, in 1949. Awarded a Doctorate of Science by Reading University in 1957, the Prince commented, 'It must be pretty well known that I never earned an honest degree in my life and I certainly never made any effort to gain an honorary one.'

Despite not having studied for a degree, Philip's speeches were often peppered with impressive references and hinted at a lifetime of self-education.

Accepting an award in 1960, he said, 'Some people might well feel that your Vice-Chancellor has succeeded in presenting me for this honorary degree, not just in a good light, but in a positively rosy glow of perfection. I can only imagine that he has taken Disraeli's advice that, "Everyone likes flattery, and when you come to royalty you should lay it on with a trowel."'

There were some things Philip is glad to have missed out on. In a speech at the Royal College of Art in 1955, he poked fun at academic gowns: 'I think perhaps the college should warn future honorary fellows of the ordeal that they will have to undergo in being made to wear flannel dressing gowns.'

> During his time as Chancellor of Edinburgh University, the Prince took advantage of his position to award an honorary Doctorate of Law to his old headmaster from Gordonstoun, Dr Kurt Hahn, saying, 'It cannot be given to many to have the opportunity and desire to heap honours upon their former headmaster.'

Always self-deprecating, in 2012 Prince Philip looked back over his awards. 'It's now quite a long time since I started my university career. But unlike most people, I started at the wrong end. I became Chancellor of the University of Wales in 1947 and have been going downhill ever since.'

Youthful Ambition

School visits often seem to bring out the less diplomatic – some might say, openly insulting – side of the Prince's sense of humour. At Fir Vale Comprehensive School in Sheffield, which had previously had a poor academic record, Philip turned to a group of parents in 2003 and asked, 'Were you here in the bad old days? … That's why you can't read or write, then.'

His presumably tongue-in-cheek attitude to the quality of education today was often on show. Fourteen-year-old George Barlow was thrilled when the royal couple accepted his invitation to visit his school in Romford, Essex, in 2003. It was a great honour for the teenager to meet the Queen and Prince Philip, who exclaimed, 'Ah, you're the one who wrote the letter. So you can write then?'

Again, the Prince didn't mince his words on a visit to the Space Shuttle, this time when he met thirteen-year-old aspiring astronaut Andrew Adams. 'Well, you'll never fly in it; you're too fat to be an astronaut … You could do with losing a bit of weight.'

During an Australian tour in 2002, the Queen and Prince Philip visited the Cairns School of Distance Education where the school band played the British national anthem. 'You were playing your instruments, weren't you?' the Prince quizzed them afterwards. 'Or do you have tape recorders under your seats?' Whether he was joking or truly doubtful about the children's musical talents is not clear.

> Not always 'down with the kids', when visiting Aberdeen in 2012, Prince Philip commented of a girl wearing a 'Kickers' jumper, 'I thought that said "Knickers".'

Children didn't have to be in school to be treated insensitively. With his fingers in his ears, smiling, Prince Philip told a group of deaf children standing near a Caribbean steel drum band in 2000, 'Deaf? If you're near there, no wonder you are deaf.'

Philip has also long since overcome any sense of awe when faced with visiting VIPs. In 1965, when asked by a teenager if he was nervous when meeting heads of state, the Prince replied, 'Well, it's surprising how you grow out of it.'

> It is not clear if Philip was commenting
> on the children or the ability of those looking
> after them in 1998, when he asked a primary
> school caretaker at Bootle in Merseyside, 'Can
> you manage to control all these vandals?'

'[Children] go to school because their parents don't want them in the house,' he explained in 2013, prompting giggles from Malala Yousafzai, who famously survived a Taliban assassination attempt and now campaigns for the rights of girls to go to school without fear.

He was returning to a familiar theme. At a new school opening in 2000 the Prince said, 'Holidays are curious things, aren't they? You send children to school to get them out of your hair. Then they come back and make life difficult for parents. That is why holidays are set so they are just about the limit of your endurance.'

What one doesn't understand must be complicated indeed. At least, that is the impression Philip gave in 2016, when he said to a group of children in Cardiff, 'You must have really good brains to speak Welsh.'

Referring to the deep red uniforms worn by girls at Queen Anne's School in 1998, Prince Philip's opinion was, 'It makes you all look like Dracula's daughters!'

Family Life
and Leisure

Off-duty, relaxing with his family, particularly away from the attention and demands of his everyday public life, it's possible to glimpse another side of Prince Philip. His wife may be the head of the country, but at home, Prince Philip is most definitely head of the family. According to a former member of staff, the Queen would often ask, 'What does Philip think?' When their children were young he would regularly read their bedtime stories and liked playing chase and running games with them. It was the Prince who chose their schools, favouring for his sons the traditional boarding schools he had himself attended.

The Prince used to have regular meetings with each of his children in turn where he discussed their general conduct and contributions to 'The Firm'. As a response to the problems facing the monarchy in the early 1990s, Prince Philip was instrumental in setting up the meetings of the senior members of the royal family's Way Ahead Group. 'We have to coordinate. Don't forget, at the beginning of the Queen's reign there were just one or two of us doing things, but then the children grew up ... We got them to specialise in their interests. Charles went off to the arts, Anne went off to prisons. It's about an efficient use of resources.'

The informality of the annual Balmoral barbecue is also very much down to Prince Philip. The Prince sets off in a Land Rover with trailer attached, loaded with food, drink and utensils. The standard scene sees Philip cursing as he gets the barbecue fire going while the Queen sets out the cutlery. Valuing independence well into his nineties, until 2017 the Prince could be glimpsed weaving through the London traffic at the wheel of his own, usefully anonymous, LPG-powered taxi cab.

Modern Father?

Even though he was his firstborn, not to mention the future king, Prince Philip did not cut his newborn son any more slack than anyone else. During the birth of Prince Charles in 1948, Prince Philip played squash with his private secretary and later said of his baby son, 'He looks like a plum pudding.'

The Prince understood when he could and couldn't be of help to his wife. When the Queen was giving birth to Prince Andrew in 1960, the Prince stepped in to give a speech at a Guildhall lunch hosted by the Lord Mayor: 'It is, of course, a matter of great regret to us all that the Queen cannot be here today but, as you realize, she has other matters to attend to.'

Perhaps acknowledging some of the trickier aspects of his relationship with his eldest son, Prince Philip again revealed how family dynamics tend to play out in the same way, regardless of who you are, commenting, 'He's a romantic and I'm a pragmatist. That means we do see things differently … And because I don't see things as a romantic would, I'm unfeeling.'

Playing to the Crowd

Having been in the public eye for seventy years, Prince Philip is used to a crowd. As a man who likes to make the most out of any situation and have a bit of fun, it's not surprising that sometimes he likes to put on a bit of a show.

In 1991, Prince Philip decided it was time to give up playing polo. Interviewed on Terry Wogan's show for BBC television, the broadcaster commented on the rather athletic, high-speed nature of the sport. The Prince replied, 'There comes a time in your life when you don't want to be so athletic any more, I can tell you.'

Terry Wogan then mentioned the fact that Prince Charles was still playing.

Philip chuckled, responding, 'He's still young and vigorous … He's younger than I am, funnily enough.' Warming to the audience's obvious appreciation, the Prince added, 'He may not look it …' before roaring with laughter.

On a state visit to Canada, the Prince was asked whether he knew the Isles of Scilly. A slightly bemused Philip confirmed, 'Yes … My son owns them.' Indeed, they are part of Prince Charles's Duchy of Cornwall estate.

Nicknamed 'the doughnut' in reference to its modern design, the new Government Communications Headquarters (GCHQ) in Cheltenham was opened in 2004. MP Chris Mullin asked the Prince if he thought Charles would approve of the architecture. 'Charles who?' queried Prince Philip.

Don't Hold Back

The Duke and Duchess of York's new home at Sunninghill Park came in for a great deal of criticism when it was completed in 1990. Often jokingly referred to as 'South York', Prince Philip didn't pull any punches, saying, 'It looks like a tart's bedroom.'

After the Duke and Duchess divorced, the Prince said of his former daughter-in-law, 'Her behaviour was a bit odd ... but I'm not vindictive. I don't see her because I don't see much point.'

But the Prince did think he'd seen Sarah Ferguson at a Guards' Polo Club reception in 2001. 'Good God! I can't take canapés from you – you're Fergie!' he barked at a startled red-haired waitress. He jokingly explained to his fellow guests, 'She's working anywhere for money now.'

> After a foiled kidnap attempt on Princess
> Anne in 1974, the Prince's verdict was, 'If the
> man had succeeded in abducting Anne, she would
> have given him a hell of a time while in captivity.'
> He also commented of his daughter in 1970, 'If
> it doesn't fart or eat hay, she isn't interested.'

Philip wasn't always the most complimentary of his youngest son, Prince Edward. When Edward was offered a place at Jesus College, Cambridge in spite of his less than glittering A-level results, Prince Philip is said to have exclaimed, 'What a friend we have in Jesus.'

Less than appreciative of Edward's forays into the world of entertainment, after the 'comedy terrorist' Aaron Barschak was arrested for gate-crashing Prince William's twenty-first birthday party wearing a pink dress, fake beard and turban, Prince Philip joked to guests that Edward had planned the intrusion. He was the only senior member of the family not at the party. 'It's bound to have been Edward. Only that boy could have coached such a rotten performance out of someone.'

Reflections on Life

At a dinner celebrating his eighty-seventh birthday, the Prince was seated next to Lord Browne, the former BP chief who had recently attracted a great deal of publicity about his private life. Prince Philip turned to him and casually remarked, 'I gather you've had some problems since we last met ... Don't worry, there's a lot of that in my family.'

In 2011, as he turned ninety, the Prince was more upbeat: 'I can only assume it is largely due to the accumulation of toasts to my health over the years that I am still enjoying a fairly satisfactory state of health and have reached such an unexpectedly great age.'

In 2012, Prince Philip expressed his concerns about the future of the monarchy and royal family. 'The more accessible you become, the more ordinary you become. The argument could be that if you are ordinary, what are you doing anyway?'

Oh, to be Oneself ...

Being in the limelight as a member of the royal family for so many decades is hard work, and one can forgive Prince Philip for the occasional desire to just relax, be himself and do as he pleases.

Indeed, being a royal can mean one misses out on some of the simple treats in life: 'I never see any home cooking – all I get is fancy stuff,' the Prince complained in 1987.

This hankering for a simple life with more freedom was something Philip mentioned more than once: 'I am interested in leisure in the same way that a poor man is interested in money – I can't get enough of it.'

And when asked in 2000 what he liked to do in his rare moments off, he said, 'I'm pretty idle, really.'

After a champagne reception to mark his eightieth birthday in 2001, the Queen remarked, 'I can't believe you're eighty.'

To which Philip replied, 'I'm not sure that I recommend being eighty. It's not so much the age but trying to survive these celebrations.'

When asked how he relaxed in 2006 he was very quick to reply, 'Have dinner and go to bed.' Perhaps this sentiment best summed up Philip's attitude to how he preferred to spend his time in his later years, or maybe he was just feeling his age.

Ladies' Man

In an interview with the *Daily Mail* in November 1997, just before the royal couple celebrated their Golden Wedding anniversary, the Queen's private secretary, Martin Charteris, said of Prince Philip, 'He's a man: he likes pretty girls, he loves fun. But I am absolutely certain there was nothing that would in any way have shaken that marriage.'

Given Prince Philip's reputation as a red-blooded male, his obvious liking for female company and outspoken nature it's not surprising that his comments to, and about, women have provided more than a few memorable quotes in over seventy years in the public eye. Politely these remarks could be described as ribaldly risqué and old-fashioned, or just another aspect of the Prince's plain speaking. To others they could be judged as offensively sexist gaffes, which are more than a little bigoted in some instances.

Those Rumours

Dogged by rumours of liaisons over the years, Prince Philip reacted robustly to journalist Fiammetta Rocco who questioned him in 1992 about alleged infidelities: 'Good God, woman. I don't know what sort of company you keep. Have you ever stopped to think that for the past forty years I have never moved anywhere without a policeman accompanying me? So how the hell could I get away with anything like that?'

The Prince has been linked to a number of high-profile women, but has always denied any affairs. He complained to the Queen's cousin, Pamela Hicks, 'The way the press related it, I had affairs with all these women. I might as well have and bloody enjoyed it.'

In Pamela Hicks's opinion, her cousin 'doesn't mind when he flirts. He flirts with everyone, and she [the Queen] knows it means absolutely nothing.'

The couple's Mountbatten cousin, Patricia Brabourne, also attests, 'He would never behave badly. He has always loved the Queen … He wouldn't want to do anything to hurt her.'

Interviewed by Jeremy Paxman in 2006 when he was eighty-five, Prince Philip contended, 'As far as I'm concerned, every time I talk to a woman, they say I've been to bed with her – as if she had no say in the matter. Well, I'm bloody flattered at my age to think some pretty girl is interested in me. It's absolutely cuckoo.'

An Eye for a Pretty Face

Perhaps it is Prince Philip's appreciation of an attractive woman that helped fuel some of the rumours against him.

When introduced to the acts from the Royal Variety Performance in 2007, Prince Philip commented to comedian Russell Brand about the performer standing next to him: 'She's got all the right stuff in all the right places.'

During a Diamond Jubilee visit to Bromley, in May 2012, ninety-year-old Prince Philip met twenty-five-year-old council worker

Hannah Jackson. He couldn't resist a risqué comment about her eye-catching red dress, which had a zip running down the full length of the front. 'I would get arrested if I unzipped that dress.'

Winning Women's Hearts Everywhere

Philip was no more sensitive with women than with any other sector of society, often bluntly telling them exactly what he thought. 'British women can't cook,' Prince Philip confidently announced to a packed audience of the Scottish Women's Institute in 1961, which probably wasn't one of his finest moments.

Again, his joke at a royal reception in 1987 wasn't really in the best of taste, when he quipped to a female solicitor, 'I thought it was against the law these days for a woman to solicit.'

Sometimes his comments could come across as plain rude. 'You are a woman, aren't you?' Philip asked on accepting a gift from a local woman in Kenya in 1984.

He wasn't at his most respectful, either, when he said in 1988, 'When a man opens a car door for his wife, it's either a new car, or a new wife.'

In 2009, the Prince asked twenty-four-year-old Barnstaple sea cadet Elizabeth Rendle what she did for a living. When told she worked in a nightclub, he asked, 'Do you work in a strip club?' The cadet politely answered no and explained that she was in fact a barmaid. Realizing he had probably gone too far, the Prince tried to make things better by commenting that it was 'probably too cold for that anyway'.

Visiting a women's centre in Hull in the same year he asked, 'Still downtrodden, then?' Obviously on something of a roll, later that day he met victims of the severe floods that had affected the city. As he said goodbye to the council leader, Carl Minns, he said, 'Keep your head above water!'

> There may be gaffes but the Prince could always make a woman laugh. When told a young recruit was going to become a dental nurse at RAF Kinloss in 2011, Philip grinned and joked to her, 'It'll be like pulling teeth.'

At a Buckingham Palace garden party in 2012, Philip met a pregnant guest who explained she was expecting her second child. 'I hope you can afford your hat,' he commented before moving on.

It wasn't the first time he delivered his punchline before leaving his opponent open-mouthed. The following year, meeting eighty-three-year-old former Mars factory worker Audrey Cook, the

Prince listened to how she used to cut, or strip, Mars Bars by hand before reflecting, 'Most stripping is done by hand.'

Female Politicians

Women and politics were always a winning combination for Prince Philip – he could rarely keep his comments in check when encountering a female MP.

On meeting the then Scottish Tory party leader Annabel Goldie in 2010, the Prince pointed to the Scottish Labour party leader's tartan tie, which had been especially designed for the visit of Pope Benedict XVI and said, 'That's a nice tie. Are you wearing knickers made out of that material?'

It should be noted that both the Queen and visiting Pope were listening to the conversation and Annabel Goldie herself gave as good as she got: 'I couldn't possibly comment and even if I had, I couldn't possibly exhibit them.'

The Prince also seemed to be fascinated by what groups of women politicians discussed when they got together – women's rights being his usual conclusion. Coming across some female Labour MPs at a Buckingham Palace drinks party in 2000, the eagle-eyed Prince realized their name badges all bore the title 'Ms'. 'Ah, so this is feminist corner then,' he quipped.

Never one to humour anyone if he wasn't in the mood, female politicians didn't escape any more lightly.

At a Parliamentary reception for MPs and peers, Tory MP Thérèse Coffey politely commented, 'Isn't it a lovely day, Sir?' prompting a grudging, 'So far.'

> Meeting members of San Francisco's city council in 1983, including the Mayor Dianne Feinstein, he couldn't help notice they were all female, 'Aren't there any male officials?' he asked. 'This is a nanny state.'

Safety in Numbers

Philip's desire to crash the female party became something of a theme for him. On a visit to the Archbishop of Canterbury's official residence, Lambeth Palace in 2012, Prince Philip spotted a group of female clergy, including the Very Reverend Canon Dr Frances Ward, the Dean of St Edmundsbury Cathedral, and a nun, sitting together. 'So this is the female section,' he commented. 'Are you all gathered here for protection?'

Below the Belt

An introduction to a group of middle-aged belly dancers in Swansea in 2008 could not pass without comment.

'I thought Eastern women just sat around smoking pipes and eating sweets all day,' the Prince joked.

'We do that as well,' one replied.

'I can see that.' Somehow Prince Philip got away with it and the dancers roared with laughter.

Making an unscheduled stop at Druckers Vienna Patisserie in Crawley in 2006, Prince Philip pointed at the cakes and asked the manager, 'Are you responsible for making people overweight in Crawley?'

Claire Burns, the manager, later said she thought the Prince was very funny.

It's a Cracker

On a visit to Southampton in 2015, where the Queen was to name a new cruise liner, Prince Philip was introduced to P&O's Human Resources director, Paula Porter. 'Humans are not resources!' he protested.

'I thought it was a very good line,' the company executive laughed. 'I shall be using it again.'

Stony Silence

The Prince's quips are not always met with humour.

When Canadian author Carol Shields told him she wrote about women and their problems, Prince Philip joked, 'What about men and their problems?' Failing to get a response, he was determined to continue: 'On second thoughts, there isn't much to say. They've only got one problem and that's women.'

While attending a medieval fair in Windsor, Prince Philip noticed a woman dressed in period costume breast-feeding her baby away from the crowds.

'What are you doing, m'lady?' he enquired loudly. To fill the growing silence he made matters even worse by adding, 'Oh look everyone, she's really taken the part to heart and is breast-feeding her child.'

Damsels in Distress

Philip could also play the knight in shining armour. While on a family holiday in a remote area of Ross-shire in Scotland in the 1970s, Prince Philip was driving along a country road with Rob Tweddle, a naturalist from the Inverpolly Nature Reserve.

Tweddle later wrote, 'We came across a green Morris Minor that had run off the road. The offside wheels had gone into a ditch. Two female teachers were standing at the side of the road. I stopped the car and Philip jumped out and we actually lifted the car back on to the road.

Philip said to them, "Now don't do that again," and we got back in the car. When I looked back they were still standing with their mouths open.'

The Prince
and the Press

P rince Philip was the first senior member of the royal family to take part in a television interview, when he spoke to Richard Dimbleby in May 1961. He also famously invited the cameras behind the scenes at the Palace to film the documentary *Royal Family* in 1969. However, Prince Philip's verbal jousts with the Fourth Estate have not always been so friendly, and both the Prince and the Queen are said to have later regretted allowing the 1969 film, which has not been shown in full for many years. When you consider what the royal family have had to contend with over the decades, from gross invasions of privacy, salacious stories, phone taps, illicit photographs, public humiliations and even undercover reporters posing as Palace staff, it is not surprising that journalists have sometimes borne the brunt of the Prince's biting wit and anger.

Cold Blooded

Prince Philip's attitude towards the press was apparent very early on. Initially fairly open-minded, he became increasingly cynical. He was infuriated by newspaper speculation of a rift between himself and the Queen during his six-month solo tour of the Commonwealth during the winter of 1956 to 1957. Official statements to the contrary only fanned the flames and the gossip continued.

'Well, you have mosquitoes, we have the press,' he commented to the matron of a Caribbean hospital during a 1968 visit.

And leaving little doubt of the strength of his animosity, he said of the press, 'invasion of privacy, invention and false quotations are the bane of our existence ... We have found that short of starting libel proceedings, there is absolutely nothing to be done.'

> The Prince even had a nickname for his foes. Attending a cocktail party in the garden of a government building in Bangladesh, in 1983, the Prince was overheard to say to the Queen, 'Here come the bloody reptiles!' as the press arrived.

'Who the hell are you?' the Prince demanded of a reporter taking notes at a Small Business Association lunch in 1969.

'I'm John Shaw of the Press Association,' the journalist replied.

Prince Philip was definitely not impressed. 'What the hell are you doing here? No one told me the press was going to be here. This is disgraceful. I'm off.'

Candid Camera

Nevertheless, moments of unguarded candour when dealing with the press have stirred up a great deal of controversy at times. Prince Philip was obviously in an expansive mood on a state visit with the Queen to the USA in November 1969.

Interviewed by NBC's Barbara Walters, who asked him, 'Might Queen Elizabeth ever abdicate and turn the throne over to Prince Charles?' Prince Philip answered flippantly, 'Who can tell? Anything might happen.' He was being less than serious, but his remarks were splashed across the British press the following day, unleashing a huge outpouring of support for the Queen from the general public.

Barbara Walters apologized to the Prince for the ensuing chaos, but he was remarkably cheerful and wrote that he was happy this had been the 'means of unlocking such a spectacular display of cheerfulness and goodwill … particularly in this day and age when most demonstrations seem to reflect nothing but anger and provocation.'

Perhaps this encouraged him. Interviewed on NBC's *Meet the Press* a few days later, the Prince was no more careful in his responses. Asked how the royal family was coping with inflation, he replied, 'We go into the red next year. Now, inevitably, if nothing happens we shall either have to – I don't know – we may have to move into smaller premises. Who knows? … We had a small yacht which we had to sell.'

Interviewed at an American Press Corps lunch in London in 2000, the Prince shared a story about a trip he had made to the US some years earlier.

'I was told for this trip I needed a PR chap to advise. So they produced this fellow – I can't remember what he was called, "Rogers" or something like that, lovely man – and he said would I see him before I left. And so he came along, and I said, "What do you want me to do?" and he said, "You've got to get along with the media."

'I said, "What sort of thing do you expect? I'm not having a press conference getting out of an airplane, I can tell you that." He said, "Oh, they're very intelligent, the US press, they're not as crude as they are in this country." And I said, "Well, okay, if that's what you think, but I tell you one thing: the first question I'm asked when I get to these things is, "Say, Prince, how do you like America?"

'So, he fell about laughing. I then arrived in Miami and was taken into a darkened room where there were about sixty-four of these microphone things in front of me, and it was pitch dark, so I couldn't see a soul in the place, and he then announced I would take answers.

'The very first question was, "Say, Prince, whaddya think of America?"'

Newspapers

If you're a royal, reading the paper is a sure-fire way to find out what the press think of you. Yet Prince Philip tends to be a discerning reader. 'I don't read the tabloids,' he told Jeremy Paxman in 2006. 'I glance at one [broadsheet]. I reckon one's enough. I can't cope with them. But the Queen reads every bloody paper she can lay her hands on.'

This hasn't always been the case for Philip. In the earlier years of the Queen's reign the Prince's biographer, Tim Heald, wrote that Philip used to check every newspaper at breakfast, saying, 'Let's see what I'm supposed to have done wrong yesterday.'

The Prince reserves a particular level of vitriol for the *Sun*'s owner Rupert Murdoch. In 2006, his comment on the media mogul was damning: 'His anti-establishment views really pulled the plug on an awful lot of things that we hold to be quite reasonable and sensible institutions.'

And when asked what had marked the general downturn in newspaper quality, he had no hesitation, replying, 'After Rupert Murdoch bought the *Today* newspaper.'

Not surprising, then, that at a fundraising event in 2003, on being told that a journalist was from the *Sun*, Prince Philip's dismissive response was, 'Oh no ... One can't tell from the outside.'

He is also said to have made the same comment about the *Daily Mirror* editor, Piers Morgan.

Philip's ire was not only directed at Murdoch. In 1962, after it had published a run of revealing royal stories, he complained, 'The *Daily Express* is a bloody awful newspaper ... full of lies, scandal and imagination ... a vicious newspaper.'

In the 1990s he commented, 'Day after day there was a derogatory story about one member of the family or another.'

The Prince bemoaned that newspapers only ever printed the bad, not the good. 'People only want to know about the splashy things, or the scandalous things. They're not really interested in anything else. What you want is a *Dynasty* production where everybody can see what we do privately.'

Philip commented to President Jacques Chirac of France in 1996, 'If we had your laws, the British press could not have done so much damage to the royal family.'

Three years later, he complained that 'The press have turned us into a soap opera.'

Even so, the Prince was never one to take himself too seriously or fail to see the humorous side of things. He has a collection of press cartoons of himself hanging on his lavatory walls at Sandringham.

Blithering Idiots

Anyone in the media was fair game, as far as Philip was concerned, who viewed them all with disdain.

At a film premiere in 1996, on meeting Sir Michael Bishop, then chairman of Channel 4, the Prince exclaimed, 'So you're responsible for the kind of crap Channel 4 produces!'

And after being informed by BBC journalist Michael Buerk, in 2004, that he knew about the Duke of Edinburgh Gold Awards, Prince Philip failed to be impressed and returned with the put-down, 'Well, that's more than you know about anything else, then.'

These derogatory comments were nothing new. 'You bloody load of clots. You could take pictures like this any Sunday at home at Windsor,' he berated news photographers at a polo match in Jamaica in 1966.

Even if the media's questions weren't aimed at him, he could be quick to involve himself. 'Damn fool question!' the Prince snapped at Caroline Wyatt, reporting for the BBC at a banquet in the Elysée Palace, in 2006. The journalist had dared to ask the Queen if she was enjoying her visit to Paris.

Stating the Bleeding Obvious

While he struggled with the media in general, the Prince had particularly little patience when asked an obvious question.

Leaving hospital after treatment for a bladder infection contracted during the Queen's Diamond Jubilee celebrations, Prince Philip was asked if he was feeling better. 'Well, I wouldn't be coming out if I wasn't,' he pointed out, reasonably enough.

In 2005, when a reporter made the mistake of asking, 'I wonder if you might like to talk to me?' Prince Philip replied briskly, 'Well, you can carry on wondering.'

When asked by a journalist if he would care to give his opinion of the new British Embassy in Berlin, which was opened by the Queen in 2000, Prince Philip was brief and to the point: 'No.'

He later condemned the £18 million building as 'a vast waste of space'.

Damned Republicans

Spotting known republican editor in chief of the *Independent* Simon Kelner at a Windsor Castle press reception to celebrate the Golden Jubilee in 2002, Prince Philip asked him what he thought he was doing there. On being told that Philip had himself sent the invitation, the Prince retorted snappily, 'Well, you didn't have to come!'

Thumb Twiddling

Showing he both read what was written and took it to heart, an article in the *Daily Mirror* of 1954 claimed the royal family had nothing better to do than stay at home and 'twiddle their thumbs'. On a visit to the Ford Dunlop factory in Birmingham shortly after, Prince Philip joked ironically, 'Of course, ladies and gentlemen, you know what I am doing, I am twiddling my thumbs.'

Reassuring

Prince Philip could also show reporters a softer side to his character.

'I don't grill newsmen for breakfast,' he said reassuringly in 1965.

Following directions from his newspaper, a photographer was told to take photographs of Prince Philip as he arrived at Aberdeen Airport and then again when he left later in the day. It was freezing cold and the photographer had been waiting around for hours when the Prince finally reappeared.

'Has my face changed that much in twelve hours?' mocked Philip.

The photographer, by then thoroughly miserable, cold and bored, couldn't help snapping, 'F*** you!' Always a fan of straight talking, the Prince took pity on the poor man and went across to talk to him.

Offensive

Caught at the wrong moment, Philip would be openly hostile. 'Here comes that bloody machine again … Why don't you stick it up your …!' he snarled to approaching television reporters carrying a microphone at London Airport in 1966.

And, on occasion, he could be quite heartless. When an over-ambitious press photographer fell out of a tree during a royal visit to India, the Prince was less than sympathetic, commenting, 'I hope to God he breaks his bloody neck.'

He has been making jokes at the expense of the press since shortly after he entered the public stage. Looking at the Barbary apes on a visit to the Rock of Gibraltar in 1950, accompanied by the usual posse of press, Prince Philip couldn't help joking, 'Which are the apes and which are the reporters?'

It's not just English journalists that have been at the receiving end of the Prince's ire, he can also be insulting in French: '*Vous êtes fous. Restez chez vous.*' Which translates as: You are crazy. Go home.

Losing Patience

When he did give the press some of his time, he wanted them to use it wisely.

'Just take the f***ing picture!' he shouted at a photographer who was taking a little too long to snap an official photo at the RAF Club, for an event marking the seventy-fifth anniversary of the Battle of Britain, in 2015.

And when reporters and photographers got too close to the Queen on an official visit, he was quick to tell them to back off. 'Don't jostle the Queen!'

He has also been known to take advantage of a panic button in his pocket, instantly summoning the police to come running to his aid, to put off approaching journalists.

Surprise!

Covering a royal visit to Malta, in 2007, celebrating the Queen and Prince Philip's sixtieth wedding anniversary, reporter Romilly Weeks had trouble keeping a straight face as she filmed a live report for ITN.

A playful Prince Philip crept up behind her and tried to distract her. At the end he yelled, 'Finished?' The reporter jumped, then dissolved into fits of laughter.

Less good-humoured was an encounter with *Sun* photographer Arthur Edwards in 1980. The cameraman was unaware that Prince Philip had spotted him sitting in his car near to the stables on the Sandringham estate. 'Having a good snoop?' the Prince asked loudly, suddenly appearing at the car window.

Some years later he yelled at a group of tabloid journalists and paparazzi standing near the gates to Sandringham, leaving them in no doubt of his opinion of them: 'You people are scum!'

Mellowing with Age

By the time of Fiona Bruce's BBC interview in 2011, the Prince was rather more circumspect in his attitude to the media.

'The media is a professional intruder. You can't complain about it … I don't see why people shouldn't know what's going on. Much better that they should know than speculate.'

And when asked whether he thought the press had been unfair over the years, he said, 'Yes, occasionally. But they have their own agenda and you just have to live with that.'

Philip revealed that he had developed a strategy for dealing with the media in his later years. In 2006 he claimed, 'I reckon I have done something right if I don't appear in the media. So I've retreated – quite consciously – so as not to be an embarrassment.'

He also commented, 'I don't hate the press. I find a lot of it is very unpalatable. But if that's the way they want to behave, well …'

> In 1999, he summed up his image in the press simply: 'There we are. I've become a caricature. I've just got to live with it.'

Avoid Where Possible

The old adage 'Never discuss politics or religion' is perhaps particularly true for Prince Philip, whose every utterance tends to be reported. But in the sort of role he's fulfilled over the past seven decades it would have been impossible for him to avoid politicians, statesmen and clergy of all faiths. So what's a man to do – keep silent? That's not exactly the Prince's style and, as a result, we have some fairly colourful quotes on record.

POLITICS ...

Prince Philip's earliest brushes with politicians were not the easiest. He had generally been viewed with suspicion and had not been the number-one choice for husband of the heir to the throne. He was seen as too liberal and more left-leaning politically than the traditional royals. His potential influence over the future Queen was feared. There had also been the controversy over Philip's surname, with Prime Minister Winston Churchill insisting that even his adopted Mountbatten was not appropriate for the royal children, who were to retain the Queen's surname, Windsor. Philip's suggestion of Edinburgh-Windsor was also vetoed. Harold Macmillan wrote in his diary on the subject that although 'this has been a painful episode … it is a very good thing that the influence of the Consort and his family should have had an early rebuff.'

A Spare Part

It quickly became apparent upon Elizabeth's ascension that none of the officials had a clue what the young consort to the sovereign was supposed to do. More than once Philip was made to feel irrelevant.

'Constitutionally I don't exist,' he commented.

On Politicians

Prince Philip was reflecting what many people think when it comes to politicians making sense. 'To understand what ministers are sometimes saying you must buy a gobbledegook dictionary and add an arbitrary ten years to every promise they make,' he said in 1960.

> In his book *Men, Machines and Sacred Cows*, Prince Philip writing in 1984 explained, 'I have no sympathy with people who claim to know what is good for others.'

On being told that Ghana had 200 MPs, Prince Philip approved. 'That's about the right number,' he said. 'We have six hundred and fifty and most of them are a complete bloody waste of time.'

Yet on a trip to Paraguay in 1963, he didn't appear to think much more of citizen rule than of politicians. 'It's a pleasure to be in a country that isn't ruled by its people,' he told Paraguayan dictator General Alfredo Stroessner.

Open and Honest

The Prince seems to have taken to heart the idea of 'speaking truth to power'. 'You're just a silly little Whitehall twit; you don't trust me and I don't trust you,' was how he summed up their relationship to Sir Rennie Maudslay, Keeper of the Privy Purse, in 1970.

And he was always happy to voice his opinion. 'Ghastly place, isn't it?' was Prince Philip's verdict on Stoke-on-Trent after meeting the Labour MP for the town, Joan Walley, at a reception in 1997.

Prince Philip has been quoted as saying of Tony Blair, 'He promises education, education, education, but never delivers' and is said to have exclaimed rather graphically, 'Well, bugger me with a ragman's trumpet!' on being told of Blair's re-election as prime minister in 2005. Tony Blair's wife, Cherie, however, came to 'have a soft spot for Prince Philip', with whom she shared an interest in the internet and new technology.

When asked by his biographer, Gyles Brandreth, if he was a modernizer, the Prince was adamant: 'No, not for the sake of modernizing, like some bloody Blairite, not for the sake of buggering about with things.'

Prince Philip is said to have never forgiven Tony Blair for the decision to scrap the royal yacht *Britannia*, which was decommissioned in 1997. Speaking fourteen years later he said, 'She should have had her steam turbines taken out and diesel engines put in. She was sound as a bell, and she could have gone on for another fifty years.'

> Finding himself standing on a barge next to Prince Philip in 2004, Labour party spin doctor Alastair Campbell was uncharacteristically lost for words and said the first thing that came into his head. He asked the Prince if he reckoned he could drive a barge. Prince Philip turned an eagle eye on Campbell and reminded him curtly that he had been a naval Commander.

Speak Up!

Prompting rumours that the Prince might be growing rather hard of hearing in his eightieth year, at a Buckingham Palace reception, Denis MacShane, Labour MP for Rotherham, said to the Queen, 'Thank you for having us, Ma'am.'

'What did he say?' Prince Philip asked.

'He said, thank you for having us,' his wife replied.

'Ah, Harrogate. Nice place,' the Prince bafflingly added.

Actions Speak Louder Than Words

A reception for MPs, held at Buckingham Palace in 2002, prompted a lively exchange. Meeting new MP Parmjit Dhanda, Prince Philip asked what he had done before entering Parliament. Hearing that the politician had been a student and trade union official, the Prince was dismissive, saying, 'You didn't do anything then.'

Dhanda responded, 'What did you do before becoming Duke of Edinburgh?'

'I served in the Royal Navy during the war,' the Prince replied, smiling broadly.

Accounts differ as to whether or not this was accompanied by a one- or two-fingered gesture. The Palace denied that the Prince would have done any such thing. Dhanda himself claimed Prince Philip raised one finger and explained, 'He had a big smile on his face and it was very much in a sense of fun.'

Who Are You?

Prince Philip has seen politicians come, go, and sometimes come again during his time as the Duke of Edinburgh. So it is hardly surprising he may struggle to recall every one he has met.

At another Buckingham Palace reception, to thank everyone involved in the Diamond Jubilee celebrations of 2012, Prince Philip failed to recognize the Health Secretary, Jeremy Hunt.

'Who are you?' he asked.

On being told that the Conservative MP was now Secretary for Health but had been Culture Secretary during the Jubilee and London Olympics, Prince Philip looked singularly unimpressed. 'Well, they do move you people on a lot,' he commented drily as he walked away.

It was not the first time that Prince Philip had failed to recognize a politician. In 1999, he asked black politician Lord Taylor of

Warwick, 'And what exotic part of the world do you come from?' The answer was, 'Birmingham.'

North of the Border

Prince Philip was never enamoured of former Scottish National Party (SNP) leader Alex Salmond, and referred to him by the less-than-flattering nickname Wee Willie Winkie. After one visit by the politician in 2014, the Prince joked to servants, 'Have you counted the spoons?'

SNP MP John McNally fared rather better. He wrote to Prince Philip in 2016, on behalf of his mother Rosa, as the two share the same birthday, 10 June 1921. To Mrs McNally's delight, the Prince wrote back passing on his best wishes and acknowledging, 'I have to say that the older I get, the less I appreciate birthdays.'

Politicians Everywhere

You might expect the Prince would be slightly more careful with foreign politicians. This was not always the case. The Prince could have sparked a diplomatic incident when he insisted on greeting German Chancellor Helmut Kohl as '*Reichskanzler*' in Hanover in 1997. This was the title Adolf Hitler had adopted as Chancellor of the Third Reich.

In 2009, on being told by US President Obama that he had breakfasted with the leaders of the UK, Russia and China, Prince Philip quipped, 'And can you tell the difference between them?'

... AND RELIGION

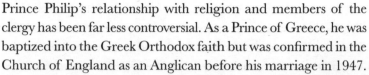

Prince Philip's relationship with religion and members of the clergy has been far less controversial. As a Prince of Greece, he was baptized into the Greek Orthodox faith but was confirmed in the Church of England as an Anglican before his marriage in 1947.

George Carey, the former Archbishop of Canterbury, said of the Prince, 'His approach is much more restless than the Queen, more focused on the intellectual side. He is searching, and he has been a bridge builder, putting faiths together. He has more time to do that, and the Queen stands back and lets him.' One of his initiatives was the Inter-Faith Dialogue between Christians, Jews and Muslims, which he set up alongside Crown Prince Hassan of Jordan and Sir Evelyn Rothschild.

Perhaps that explains Prince Philip's comment, 'I suppose I challenge things to stimulate myself and to be stimulating. You don't have to agree with everyone all the time.'

However, he always faced opposition. 'I take an interest in comparative religion but if I talk about it I'm labelled a crank,' he also claimed in 1999.

Smells and Bells

While Philip clearly has a healthy respect for religion and its practitioners, his sense of humour rears its head even in the most holy of places and occasions.

As Prince Philip and the Queen walked down the aisle of a high Anglican church in 2004 at a service to celebrate her birthday service, Philip hissed through the clouds of holy smoke, 'Is this a celebration or a cremation?'

In the same year, pausing for a moment before leaving a reception following the distribution of the Maundy Money and also celebrating the centenary of Liverpool Cathedral, the Prince tucked a couple of cans of brown ale into his inside jacket pocket. He joked that they were 'for the onward journey'.

And his considered verdict on over-long church sermons was, 'The mind cannot absorb what the backside cannot endure.'

> 'I'll tell you a secret,' Prince Philip whispered cheekily to the Roman Catholic Archbishop of Malta in 2015, who looked equally amused, 'We are all Christians.'

Speaking in the House of Lords in 2011, John Sentamu, Archbishop of York, paid tribute to Prince Philip on his ninetieth birthday. 'Not everyone is aware that His Royal Highness has a keen interest in theological questions. Bishops who are invited to stay and preach at Sandringham face a barrage of serious theological questions over lunch, and there is nowhere to hide. He listens appreciatively but never uncritically. In my case, the sermon was based on Jesus turning water into wine at Cana of Galilee.

'The Duke suggested many possible explanations for the miracle, including a Uri Geller-type explanation, and he produced a spoon which Uri Geller had bent for him. To my rescue came that still small voice of calm from Her Majesty the Queen, saying, "Philip and his theories ..."'

Prince Philip had previously tried to trick Archbishop Sentamu, who was visiting Windsor Castle. The Prince showed him a charred beam from the fire there in 1992 and pretended that it was an example of his own efforts in modern sculpture.

The Archbishop also told the story of the Bishop of Norwich's visit to Sandringham as a guest preacher. When Bishop Graham James arrived, Prince Philip asked, 'Are you happy clappy?' to which the Bishop quickly replied, 'No, I'm smells and bells.' After which the Prince and the Bishop got along very well.

> On board the Royal Yacht *Britannia* when it docked at the Pier Head in Liverpool in 1977, Prince Philip was standing with the Queen next to the Bishop of Liverpool, David Sheppard. When the brass band began playing 'The Lord is My Shepherd', Prince Philip whispered, 'Bishop, they're playing your tune.'

A Word of Caution

On occasion, Prince Philip has also been less than patient with leaders of the Church. Talking to the economist Lord Harris of High Cross, the subject of Samuel Smiles's famous 'bible of mid-Victorian liberalism', *Self Help*, led the Prince to comment, 'I think you should arrange for every bishop in the country to have a copy. They all seem to confuse self-help and individual responsibility with selfishness.'

He also spoke about the clergy to *The New York Times* in 1984: 'Almost without exception they preach peace, good will and the brotherhood of man, and yet many of them have been used by the unscrupulous to cause more human conflict and misery than any other system, save perhaps Communism.'

Public Bloomers

Famously outspoken, the Prince has met with a long list of celebrities over the years and responded with a string of well-publicized pronouncements on public figures and members of the entertainment industry. He feels no need to massage anyone's ego and, as we know, is not afraid to voice his opinions, although sometimes his failure to recognize celebrities can be just as damning. To be fair to the Prince, his criticisms are often accompanied by a telling twinkle in his eye and many people comment upon how charming and funny he is.

Singers

Singers were particularly easy targets for Prince Philip.

Attending the premiere of the James Bond film *Die Another Day* at the Royal Albert Hall, in 2002, Philip was told that Madonna would be singing the theme song. He turned to the Queen and asked, 'Are we going to need ear plugs?'

Volume is clearly one of the Prince's bugbears. Prince Philip thoroughly approved of tenor Russell Watson's rousing rendition of 'Jerusalem' at a Buckingham Palace charity fundraiser in 2011, but afterwards he asked, 'Good lord, why have you got a microphone? They can hear you in space with that voice.' He then turned to Louise Harris, the singer's partner, and added, 'You must go deaf listening to him all the time.'

He isn't always as positive about singers' voices.

When the Prince met the popular mezzo-soprano Katherine Jenkins in 2006, he asked slightly randomly, 'How are your vocal cords?'

She replied, 'Fine, thank you.'

But this was not enough detail for Prince Philip who continued, 'No boils or warts on them yet?'

Just before the Canadian quartet The Tenors performed at a Diamond Jubilee celebration at Windsor Castle, Prince Philip said encouragingly, 'I hope your voices don't break in the show.' All four were in their twenties.

Royal Variety

Prince Philip attended his first Royal Variety Performance with the Queen in 1952 and has sat through rather a lot of the shows in the years since. It is a tradition that the royals meet the performers backstage afterwards.

Although photographs from the 1969 show reveal the pair laughing together and sharing a joke, Prince Philip was less than complimentary about Tom Jones.

'What do you gargle with – pebbles?' the Prince asked the singer.

Thinking further, Philip later commented the next day, 'It is very difficult at all to see how it is possible to become immensely valuable by singing what I think are the most hideous songs.'

He does not seem to have revised his opinion. Attending a small-business lunch when the subject was raised of how hard it was to make a fortune in Britain, Prince Philip asked, 'What about Tom Jones? He's made a million and he's a bloody awful singer.'

Elton John also came in for his fair share of derision. When he began his set at the 2001 Variety show, the Queen said to Philip, 'I wish he'd turn his microphone to the side.' The Prince had a better suggestion: 'I wish he'd turn his microphone off!'

This was not the only time that year that the Prince was rather insulting to the singer-songwriter, who is a near neighbour of the royal couple, as he also owns a house in Windsor. Hearing that Elton John had sold his Watford Football-club themed Aston Martin, Prince Philip exclaimed, 'Oh, it's you that owns that ghastly car, is it? We often see it when driving to Windsor Castle.'

> In November 2003, the Royal Variety
> Performance was staged in Edinburgh for the
> first time, with the Queen and Prince Philip
> attending. Afterwards, when he came to greet
> Donny Osmond, former teen idol of the 1970s, the
> Prince joked, 'Will someone please give some grey
> hair to this kid?' The singer was then forty-five,
> though he still looked remarkably youthful.

After the 2007 Performance, Prince Philip met Simon Cowell and Piers Morgan, judges on *Britain's Got Talent* who had appeared to introduce singer Paul Potts, their show's first winner. 'You're the judges, is that right?' the Prince asked. 'So, you sponge off him then?' he added, pointing to the singer.

Sometimes it pays to be a little more in touch with pop culture.

At the 2009 line-up, Prince Philip was introduced to members of Diversity, the multi-ethnic street dance troupe from London and Essex who had won the third series of *Britain's Got Talent* that year.

'Are you all one family?' the Prince enquired. 'Did you come over just for this one show?'

Radio Stars

The Prince is clearly not the greatest fan of the modern music industry. He made his feelings quite clear at his seventieth birthday party at Windsor Castle, in 1991, when he met Terrie Doherty. At the time Doherty was head of Sony Music Promotion in London, a role that involved dealing with radio and television producers. Hearing this, Prince Philip grimaced, 'Do you have to speak to those awful DJ chappies?'

Mic Magic

After watching the musical *Chicago* at the Adelphi Theatre in London, the Prince found himself chatting to girls from the chorus line still dressed in the skimpy costumes and fishnet stockings they had worn on stage. 'Where on earth do you keep your microphones?' Philip asked. Apparently the mics were hidden in their hair.

Modern Machines

Meeting Cate Blanchett in 2008, he failed to recognize the well-known actress, who had been nominated for two Oscars that year. He assumed she might be able to help him with his DVD player since she worked in the film industry. 'There's a cord sticking out of the back. Might you tell me where it goes?' he asked her.

The following year he gave full vent to his irritation with television sets: 'To work out how to operate a TV set you practically have to make love to the thing. They put the controls on the bottom so you have to lie on the floor, and then if you want to record something the recorder is underneath, so you end up lying on the floor with a torch in your teeth, a magnifying glass and an instruction book. Either that or you have to employ a grandson of age ten to do it for you.'

Film Fun

After watching the premiere of *The Voyage of the Dawn Treader*, the third film in the Chronicles of Narnia series, in 2010, the Queen and Prince Philip met members of the cast and crew. When he came to Simon Pegg, who was the voice of Reepicheep, the swashbuckling mouse, the Prince asked the actor, 'When did you first realize you had the voice of a mouse?'

Reality TV

The Prince wasn't any more a fan of reality television than he was a follower of entertainment shows, it seems. He had clearly never watched the Channel 4 series *Gogglebox* and had no idea who regulars Sandra Martin or Sandy Channer were when he was introduced to them in 2016. They duly explained what the show was all about. Prince Philip did not find the idea appealing: 'Well, I won't be watching you, that's for sure.'

Table Matters

In 1990, when actor David Suchet received an invitation to lunch with the Queen and Prince Philip at Buckingham Palace on his forty-fourth birthday, at first he thought it was a hoax. At the end of the meal, Suchet selected a mango from the fruit bowl and, realizing he had no idea how to peel it in 'polite company', he turned to the Prince for advice.

'You don't peel a mango, you slice it,' Philip explained, and proceeded to take another mango and demonstrate exactly what to do.

Suchet decided to use the 'mango incident' in his next Poirot episode, 'The Theft of the Royal Ruby'. 'There is even a joke about it in the film itself,' the actor said. 'When one of the dinner guests asks how Poirot knows how to treat a mango, the screenwriter Anthony Horowitz wrote the line, "A certain duke taught me."'

After watching the musical comedy *Betty Blue Eyes*, which was based on the film *A Private Function*, and set in 1947, Prince Philip met members of the cast. Among them was Annalisa Rossi, who had played the young Princess Elizabeth. 'You remind me of somebody,' he joked. Moving on to the actor Dan Burton, who had played him on stage, the Prince commented, 'I like the hair.'

Try Harder Next Time

The Prince is an admirer of a proper beard, despite being himself clean-shaven. Philip was unimpressed by Stephen Judge's tiny goatee beard at a Buckingham Palace reception in 2009, especially when he learned that Judge was a designer. The Prince scolded him, 'Well, you didn't design your beard too well, did you? You really must try better with your beard.'

He was equally underwhelmed by composer Simon Bainbridge's beard, which he considered rather sparse, particularly in comparison with his hair. Meeting him at the Royal Academy, the Prince asked, 'Why don't you go the whole hog?'

Food for Thought

Not thinking through what he is about to say is one of Philip's trademarks, and, as a result, his words can often be taken the wrong way.

Offered fish to sample at Rick Stein's seafood deli in 2000, the Prince was blunt: 'No, I would probably end up spitting it out over everybody.'

This was afterwards explained to be a comment on the difficulties of eating fish while walking around, rather than a comment on its quality or taste. The celebrity chef has cooked for the Queen and Prince Philip on a number of other occasions.

When Phillip Met Prince Philip: 60 Years of the Duke of Edinburgh Award

In December 2016, presenter Phillip Schofield interviewed Prince Philip for a television programme to mark the sixtieth anniversary of the Duke of Edinburgh Award Scheme. It has to be said that the Prince is not the easiest of interviewees and on being told that Schofield was going to take part in a wing walk to raise funds for the scheme he appeared unimpressed, quipping, 'Who is trying to get rid of you?'

Prince Philip continued, 'Are you going to stand there on the wing and say, "Hello folks"? I wouldn't open your mouth if I were you ... You'll blow up like a balloon.'

A few days later, when the Prince invited the presenter to the Palace, Schofield assumed it was something to do with the programme. Instead, Prince Philip introduced him to a parachutist, joking, 'Meet a fellow idiot!'

Smuggling Opportunities

When Prince Philip met Adam Hills, the Australian comedian and host of TV show *The Last Leg*, who was born without a right foot and has a prosthetic limb, the comedian spoke about his plans to return to Australia. The Prince joked back, 'You could smuggle a bottle of gin out of the country in that artificial foot.'

Hills told the *Daily Mirror* he thought the line was 'brilliant'.

Portraits Never Lie

'Gadzooks! Why have you given me a great schonk?' Prince Philip exclaimed on seeing a portrait of himself by Stuart Pearson Wright in 2004. It shows him bare-chested, with a bluebottle fly on his shoulder, green shoots sprouting from his index finger and with a disproportionately large nose. It's title, *Homo sapiens, Lepidium sativum and Calliphora vomitoria*, means 'A wise man, some cress and a bluebottle'.

As far as the bare chest goes, the artist admitted, 'It's not his, though. He didn't get his chest out for me. I was going to ask him, but I didn't get around to it.'

The Royal Society for the Encouragement of Arts, Manufactures and Commerce, which originally commissioned the portrait to mark the fiftieth anniversary of Prince Philip as its president, rejected it as 'inappropriate'. The Prince sat for four one-hour sessions with the artist before relations broke down. After the final one, Pearson Wright dared to ask if his royal subject thought he'd captured a likeness. 'I bloody well hope not!' Philip quickly replied.

Prince of Non-PC

In his collection of essays, speeches and lectures, *Men, Machines and Sacred Cows*, Prince Philip observed, 'Trying to be funny is a great deal more difficult than trying to be serious. What may strike me as a witty comment can easily turn out to be painfully tactless.'

Alan Titchmarsh once asked Prince Philip if he regretted having been so famously blunt. 'Well, yes,' Philip conceded. 'I would rather not have made the mistakes I did make, but I'm not telling you what they were.'

Below are a few of the comments that he really would have been wiser not to make.

On Overpopulation

Becoming enthused by one of his favourite topics, the need for birth control to tackle the problems of overpopulation, and more specifically multi-coloured condoms in Thailand, the Prince suggested, 'They choose yellow if they are happy and black if they are in mourning.'

Terror Attack

Meeting a young female police officer wearing a bulletproof vest on Stornoway, Isle of Lewis, in 2002, the Prince joked, 'You look like a suicide bomber.'

A Matter of Taste

In 2002, fifteen-year-old army cadet Stephen Menary, who had been blinded in an IRA bombing, was invited to a tree-planting ceremony in Hyde Park. The Queen asked the teenager how much vision he still had. The Prince, in a very audible aside, answered, 'Not a lot, judging by the tie he's wearing.'

A stunned silence greeted this remark. Even the normally impassive Queen stared at her husband open-mouthed.

Safety First

Context can be everything. On the subject of smoke alarms, he said they were, 'A damn nuisance – I've got one in my bathroom and every time I run my bath the steam sets it off.' This might have been fine apart from the fact that he voiced this opinion to a woman whose two sons had died in a fire in 1998.

Cowboys and Indians

Speaking out of turn in Scotland in August 1999, Prince Philip's verdict on an old-fashioned electrical fuse box was, 'It looks as though it was put in by an Indian.'

This was too great a gaffe even for the Prince and he later tried to correct his comment. 'I meant to say cowboy. I just got my cowboys and Indians mixed up.'

Outrageously Inappropriate

Cultural rights and the identity of indigenous people are never good subjects for humour, and for someone as well read and widely travelled as Prince Philip it should have been obvious he needed to proceed with caution. It's hard to know why he would ever think this comment was a wise idea.

'Do you still throw spears at each other?' Prince Philip asked, shocking Aboriginal leader and successful entrepreneur William Brin, when visiting the Aboriginal Cultural Park in Queensland, Australia, in 2002.

> 'Do you know they're now producing eating dogs for anorexics?' he joked to a blind woman standing with her guide dog outside Exeter Cathedral in 2002.

Enough Said

There have also been the jokes that embarrassingly misfired.

'They're not mating, are they?' he asked as two robots bumped in to one another at the Science Museum in London, in 2000.

The Prince may have made many good puns over the years, but not on this occasion. 'A pissometer?' This was Philip's attempt to rename the piezometer, the water gauge for measuring water pressure, which was being demonstrated by Australian farmer Steve Filelti in 2000.

Fond Farewell

On Wednesday 2 August 2017, Prince Philip made his final solo public engagement. It was fitting that his last official royal event should have been a Royal Marines Parade, where he met servicemen who had taken part in a 1664-mile Global Challenge trek to raise funds for and awareness of the Royal Marines Charity. The Prince is their Captain General.

At the age of ninety-six, the Prince looked cheerful and still cut a striking figure as he walked across the forecourt of Buckingham Palace wearing his signature raincoat and a bowler hat as protection against the rain. Unsurprisingly, he couldn't resist a wisecrack. 'You should all be locked up!' he joked in reference to the Marines' fundraising.

He met two corporals who ran 1664 miles over 100 days and chatted to Lieutenant Colonel Aldei Alderson, who ran 100 kilometres in full uniform and polished army boots.

The Plymouth Band struck up a rousing rendition of 'For He's a Jolly Good Fellow' as the Prince inspected the Marines at the Captain General's Parade. He tipped his hat to the troops and waved before walking back inside Buckingham Palace.

Since his wife became Queen in 1952, Prince Philip has carried out 22,219 solo engagements and even in his retirement year was still among the most active royals. Palace records suggest he made his first solo engagement on 2 March 1948, just a few months after his marriage, when he attended the London Federation of Boys' Clubs boxing finals at the Royal Albert Hall. Almost seventy years before his retirement, the Prince, then aged just twenty-six, awarded the prizes.

Speaking on the *Today* programme on BBC Radio 4, Lady Myra Butter, who has known Prince Philip since childhood, said, 'I'm sure he won't disappear; he will be greatly missed by everybody. He's been such a stable character in all our lives – he's always there and he's always been there for the Queen and I think we're very, very lucky to have him.'

Prince Edward also commented that he didn't think his father would be 'disappearing into the background', and indeed, the Prince may still attend certain official events alongside the Queen.

'It's better to get out before you reach the sell-by date'

Despite his continued busy schedule well into his nineties, the Prince had anticipated his retirement back in 2011 when interviewed for the BBC on the eve of his ninetieth birthday.

'I reckon I've done my bit. I want to enjoy myself for a bit now. With less responsibility, less frantic rushing about, less preparation, less trying to think of something to say. On top of that your memory's going. I can't remember names. Yes, I'm just sort of winding down.'

Irreverent as ever, at a Buckingham Palace event following the announcement of his retirement, Prince Philip told restaurateur, writer and broadcaster Prue Leith, 'I'm discovering what it's like to be on your last legs. But while you're still alive you might as well keep moving, or try to.'

Bibliography

Arscott, David, *Queen Elizabeth II: Diamond Jubilee 60 Years a Queen: A Very Peculiar History*, Book House, 2012

Bedell Smith, Sally, *Elizabeth The Queen: The Life of a Modern Monarch*, Penguin Books, 2012

Botham, Noel and Montague, Bruce, *The Book of Royal Useless Information*, John Blake Publishing, 2012

Brandreth, Gyles, *Philip and Elizabeth: Portrait of a Marriage*, Arrow Books, 2004

Butt, Antony A., *The Wisdom of Prince Philip*, Hardie Grant Books, 2015

Carey, George, *Know the Truth: A Memoir*, HarperCollins, 2004

Cawthorne, Nigel, *I Know I am Rude But it is Fun: The royals and the rest of us as seen by Prince Philip*, Gibson Square, 2016

Dampier, Phil and Walton, Ashley, *Prince Philip: Wise Words and Golden Gaffes*, Barzipan Publishing, 2012

Eade, Philip, *Young Prince Philip: His Turbulent Early Life*, HarperPress, 2011

Heald, Tim, *The Duke: A Portrait of Prince Philip*, Hodder & Stoughton, 1991

Marr, Andrew, *Diamond Queen: Elizabeth II and Her People*, Macmillan UK, 2011

Petrella, Kate, *Royal Wisdom: The Most Daft, Cheeky, and Brilliant Quotes from Britain's Royal Family*, Adams Media, 2011

Prince Philip, *Men, Machines and Sacred Cows*, Hamish Hamilton, 1984

Prince Philip, *Prince Philip Speaks: Selected Speeches 1956–1959*, Collins Clear-Type Press, 1960

Prince Philip, *Selected Speeches, 1948–1955*, Oxford University Press, 1957

Scarfe, Rory, *Do You Still Throw Spears at Each Other? 90 Years of Glorious Gaffes from the Duke*, Simon & Schuster, 2011

Interviews

'A Strange Life: Profile of Prince Philip', Fiammetta Rocco for the *Independent on Sunday*, 1992

'The Duke at Ninety', Fiona Bruce for the BBC, 2011

The Duke: A Portrait of Prince Philip, Trevor McDonald for ITV, 2008

'Duke Takes the Hazards in His Stride', Sue Mott for the *Daily Telegraph*, 2006

'I've Just Got to Live With It', Gyles Brandreth for the *Sunday Telegraph*, 1999

'Prince Philip at Ninety', Alan Titchmarsh for ITV, 2011

When Phillip Met Prince Philip: 60 Years of the Duke of Edinburgh's Award, Phillip Schofield for ITV, 2016

Websites

www.albertjack.com
www.allgreatquotes.com
www.bbc.co.uk
www.brainyquote.com

www.britroyals.com
www.crawleyobserver.co.uk
www.dailymail.co.uk
www.eonline.com
www.express.co.uk
www.facebook.com/TheBritishMonarchy
www.famousquotesandauthors.com
www.gq-magazine.co.uk
www.guardian.co.uk
www.huffingtonpost.com
www.independent.co.uk
www.inews.co.uk
www.itv.com
www.liverpoolecho.co.uk
www.mirror.co.uk
www.morefamousquotes.com
news.sky.com
www.nytimes.com
www.radiotimes.com
uk.reuters.com
www.royal.uk
www.scotsman.com
www.thesun.co.uk
www.theboltonnews.co.uk
www.telegraph.co.uk
www.telegraphindia.com
www.thinkexist.com
www.time.com
www.timesonline.co.uk
www.yorkshirepost.co.uk
www.youtube.com

Picture Credits